KINGS
AND
COMMONERS

KINGS
AND
COMMONERS

Studies in British Idealism

BY

GEORGE F. TIMPSON

Essay Index Reprint Series

 BOOKS FOR LIBRARIES PRESS
FREEPORT, NEW YORK

First Published 1936
Reprinted 1969

STANDARD BOOK NUMBER:
8369-1051-6

LIBRARY OF CONGRESS CATALOG CARD NUMBER:
70-80401

PRINTED IN THE UNITED STATES OF AMERICA

FOREWORD

THE title 'Kings and Commoners' was chosen, after much deliberation, to express that growing unity between Throne and people which has been evident during the last four reigns. Queen Victoria was deeply revered; King Edward VII came nearer to our sporting instincts, and his great kindness made him immensely popular; King George V was the Head of the Family; and our new King was our true and tried friend even before he ascended the throne.

During this century a gradual approximation of ultimate ideals has obscured the clear-cut division which once existed between the great political parties. In consequence we can no longer look to politicians for the powerful leadership which the Victorians expected and received. The issues are too confused, and varieties of opinion within the same party are too great. It has become apparent that the leadership of the nation must come from the one element which is raised above contending policies. More and more do men look to the Throne for guidance in perplexity, and for that vision without which the people perish; and by reason of its close contact with the thought

FOREWORD

and feeling of the people, the Throne is able to impart that vision in a most delicate and tender way.

This book presents a series of pictures, some grave, some gay, of men and women from all classes of the nation, and from all parts of the country. England, Scotland, Wales, Ulster, the Irishman in England, the naturalized Briton and the Jewish element are all represented. The characters depicted have been chosen for the ideals they represent, and though some are no longer with us, the work they did persists as a living element in the national life. The different chapters have been submitted to those most intimately acquainted with the subject of each, and the warm reception accorded my sketches makes me hope that they will be welcomed by the reader. I am deeply sensible of the helpfulness of all who read them, and am especially grateful for the kindness shewn to me at Buckingham Palace.

I have to thank those who have permitted me to use copyright passages : *The Christian Science Monitor* for permission to use 'The Teacher's Reward,' 'The Englishman, Lover of Flowers,' and passages in certain other chapters, all written by myself and first published in that paper ; the Executors of Edward Bowen for permission to quote from the Harrow Songs ; Messrs. Hodder and Stoughton for the quotations from Mrs. Ousey's biography of Sir John McClure ; *The Times* for the closing lines of ' King Edward as Prince ' ; the Private Secretary to His Majesty and the *Oxford Times* for the speech delivered

FOREWORD

by King Edward VIII as Prince of Wales on November 9th, 1932 ; The Oxford University Press and Elizabeth Mary Wright for the quotations from *The Life of Joseph Wright* and *The Story of Joseph Wright, Man and Scholar*. The source of the photographs is acknowledged in the list of illustrations.

I cannot close without expressing my deep indebtedness to my wife, but for whom this book would never have come into being.

GEORGE F. TIMPSON.

Maidenhill House,
Stonehouse, Glos.
July 6th, 1936.

CONTENTS

	PAGE
FOREWORD	vii

ROYAL TRIBUTES

THE GLORY AND THE MAJESTY . . . 1
The 'Last Audience' of King George V

KING EDWARD VIII AS PRINCE 6
His training and achievement

INDUSTRY

JOSIAH WEDGWOOD, THE QUEEN'S POTTER . . 11
Science, art and humanity in a light industry

SIR ALFRED YARROW 18
Science and humanity in a heavy industry

SHAPERS OF MEN

EDWARD BOWEN AND THE HARROW SONGS . 33
The foundations of modern school life

SIR JOHN MCCLURE OF MILL HILL . . . 41
A great public school finds its place : unity and goodwill in national education

THE TEACHER'S REWARD 54
The overtones of school life

CONTENTS

SPORT

	PAGE
COWES WEEK	59
Their Majesties at Cowes—*Britannia*—Thomas White Ratsey	
CRICKETERS ALL	63
D. L. Morgan—the Denton Twins—Gloucestershire—Bishop Talbot—the spirit of cricket	

DOERS AND DREAMERS

C. T. STUDD, CRICKETER AND MISSIONARY . .	71
'The set of Studds'—The Cambridge Seven—Priscilla Stewart—India—the Heart of Africa	
SIDNEY DOBELL, POET	83
International sympathy—art and life reconciled	
JOHN BELLOWS, FRIEND	91
The Traveller's Dictionary—world-wide friendships—archaeology—a great Gloucestershire figure	
COBBLERS AND KINGS	101
John Pounds—George Fox—William Carey—William Timpson	

AT HOME AND ABROAD

MASTERS OF WORDS	111
Sir James Murray and the *Oxford English Dictionary*—Joseph Wright and the *English Dialect Dictionary*	
OXFORD AND MODERN LANGUAGES . . .	121
George I and III—Sir Robert Taylor-Max Müller, Joseph Wright, H. T. Gerrans, H. G. Fiedler—King Edward VIII as Prince of Wales	
THE SERVICES	138
The Fighting and Peace Services, including the Merchant Navy—Royal leadership	

CONTENTS

'ORDINARY FELLOWS'

GARDENERS AND COUNTRY FOLK . . . 145
    H. Taylor, R. Jaques and A. Lenton—village authors in mid-Gloucestershire—the Cook and Thompson brothers

SCHOOL AND COLLEGE SERVANTS 154
    Mill Hill—Worcester College, Oxford—Wycliffe College

COUNTY MAGISTRATES 159
    T. Stops—J. Bramley—J. C. C. Kimmins—W. A. Sibly

INTERLUDE

THE SCHOOL IN THE WEST 167
    A Song of Wycliffe

THE ENGLISHMAN, LOVER OF FLOWERS . . 168

THE THREE NATIONS

THE HEART OF SCOTLAND 173
THE HEART OF WALES 177
THE HEART OF ENGLAND 180

INDEX 185

LIST OF ILLUSTRATIONS

'HIS HAPPIEST MOMENTS' . . . . . *Frontispiece*
(*By permission of Central Press Photos Ltd.*)

                                                                                                    FACING PAGE

JOSIAH WEDGWOOD 14
(*By permission of Josiah Wedgwood & Co. Ltd.*)

THE FIRST MOTOR TORPEDO BOAT, COWES, 1906   25
(*By permission of Sir Harold Yarrow, Bt.*)

EDWARD BOWEN 40
(*By permission of Longmans, Green & Co. Ltd.*)

SIR JOHN MCCLURE, LL.D., MUS.DOC. . . . 41
(*By permission of Lady McClure*)

BRITANNIA : THE LAST RACE 60
(*By permission of Beken & Son, Cowes*)

THOMAS RATSEY PRESENTING THE LUCKY SOCK TO
    MRS. FRANK ROBERTSON 61
(*From a photograph in the possession of Christopher Ratsey, Esq.*)

J. E. K., C. T. AND G. B. STUDD ; CHARLES STUDD IN
    AFRICA 82
(*By permission of the Religious Tract Society*)

LIST OF ILLUSTRATIONS

FACING PAGE

SYDNEY DOBELL 83
(*From a portrait in possession of C. Brian Dobell, Esq.,*
M.D.)

SIR JAMES MURRAY IN HIS OXFORD SCRIPTORIUM . . 114
(*By permission of the Oxford University Press*)

JOSEPH AND ELIZABETH MARY WRIGHT AND THEIR CHILDREN 115
(*By permission of Mrs. Wright and the Oxford University Press*)

PROFESSOR H. G. FIEDLER, M.V.O. 128
(*From a portrait by Lafayette*)

THE TAYLORIAN SPEECH 129
(*By permission of The Times*)

'H.M.S. WORCESTER,' by W. M. BIRCHALL (1928) . 144
(*By permission of the Captain-Superintendent of H.M.S. Worcester*)

COTSWOLD HAYMAKERS 145
(*From the coloured woodcut by J. Hall Thorpe*)

THE SCOTTISH NATIONAL WAR SHRINE: THE CASKET
PRESENTED BY KING GEORGE V AND QUEEN MARY . 176
(*By permission of Country Life Ltd.*)

KING GEORGE V AND QUEEN MARY LEAVING THE NATIONAL
MUSEUM OF WALES, 21ST APRIL, 1927 . . . 177
(*By permission of Central Press Photos Ltd.*)

NOTES ON ILLUSTRATIONS

FRONTISPIECE. King Edward VIII, as Prince of Wales, is seen responding to the greetings of Wolf Cubs and Boy Scouts. (See page 7.)

'BRITANNIA : THE LAST RACE.' Both *Britannia* and her Royal owner took part in their last race on August 10th, 1935, the final day of the Cowes Week Jubilee Regatta. The day's sport was organized by the Royal Southern Yacht Club, and proved to be the best of the Week. In twenty races *Britannia* had won no prizes, and King George V had intimated that she would not race again. On her last day there was a good breeze, and it looked for some time as though she might win, but towards the end of the race she was definitely outsailed by the 'J' class yachts, and was left to struggle with *Shamrock V* for the third or fourth place. Thus ended a career which had lasted for just over forty-two years. Since her launch at Glasgow in May, 1893, *Britannia* had secured 231 first prizes and 124 others in 589 starts. She was loved for her fine qualities as a yacht, and even more for her association with King George V. She seemed indeed to know that the end was near, and that she could never race without him. By the orders of King Edward VIII she was sunk in deep water in the Channel at midnight, July 9/10, 1936.

THE TAYLORIAN SPEECH. The persons seated immediately to right and left of H.R.H. the Prince of Wales are : (right in the photograph) the Vice-Chancellor, the President of Magdalen, the Bishop of Oxford ; (left in the photograph) Professor Fiedler (hidden by the Prince), the Master of Pembroke, Sir Charles Oman, the Junior Proctor (wearing cap).

THE SCOTTISH NATIONAL WAR SHRINE. The Shrine is the inner Sanctuary of the Scottish National War Memorial, which stands on the apex of the Castle Rock at Edinburgh. The Shrine is entered through a soaring archway from the Hall of Honour. The steel casket, presented by Their Majesties King George V and Queen Mary, contains the names of all who fell in the War. The pedestal which supports it rises from the living rock, which here pierces the granite floor of the Shrine ; above the casket the figure of St. Michael is pendant, and around it, under the seven windows, runs a great bronze frieze representing the varied types of Scottish men and women who served in the War ; even animals and carrier pigeons are included in this record. The memorial was the last work of a great Scottish architect, Sir Robert Lorimer, A.R.A., R.S.A.

ROYAL TRIBUTES

THE GLORY AND THE MAJESTY

TO that vast multitude who were privileged, after hours of patient waiting, to spend two or three minutes in 'The Last Audience' of His Majesty King George V in Westminster Hall, there was granted an impression of such solemn beauty and such deep peace as is seldom given us to experience on earth. The stately group of figures guarding the catafalque, the burning glow of glorious colour set in the great spaces of the vast hall, arrested and held the eye from the moment one arrived at the head of the stairway; but as all passed with slow footsteps down the great length of the building, the quiet reverence, the deep tenderness, the gratitude unspeakable which rose from countless hearts filled the atmosphere as with a fragrance, and stilled the troubled thought.

In the great hall which for eight and a half centuries has been the very centre of England's history, lay the last symbols of a life so lived as to demonstrate beyond all cavil the power of Christian qualities to guide and to hold together a world-wide empire. King George had been called to the throne in circumstances not wholly unlike those in which Abraham Lincoln was summoned to be President of the United States. A severe constitutional struggle was followed by the great strikes and the first stirrings of Civil

ROYAL TRIBUTES

War in Ireland. By marching into Belgium, Germany saved Britain from internal strife ; but King George, like Lincoln, essentially a man of peace, hesitated no less than he to lead his people into and through the greatest struggle of its history ; and, like Lincoln, he came out of the struggle triumphant, with the spirit of mercy and forgiveness in his heart.

During the Great War the King emerged as the true leader of the nation. Sustained by his great faith in God and in his people, he never lost heart or hope, and in the darkest hours his courage was highest. But his greatest work was yet to come. During the War, the nation had kept sternly to its high task ; after it, came the reaction. But not in the heart of the King.

Unseen except by a few, unknown to almost all, he set himself to work for ' a better Britain,' and a Britain devoted to the service of mankind. Eight days after the signing of the Armistice, he had spoken these words to a great assembly in the Royal Gallery of the Palace of Westminster :

' It is on the sense of brotherhood and mutual goodwill, on a common devotion to the common interests of the nation as a whole, that its future prosperity and strength must be built up. The sacrifices made, the sufferings endured, the memory of the heroes who have died that Britain may live, ought surely to ennoble our thoughts and attune our hearts to a higher sense of individual and national duty, and to a fuller realization of what the English-speaking race, dwelling upon the shores of all the oceans, may yet accomplish for mankind.'

—John Buchan : *The King's Grace*, p. 239.

THE GLORY AND THE MAJESTY

In the storm-tossed years which followed, the King set himself to translate those words into facts. It was a long, hard, up-hill climb. There was little to assure him that his people would realize his effort for them in peace as they had done in war. Outside of Britain, upheaval after upheaval destroyed the old order of Europe, and bitter resistance countered every forward move in India. But, supported by his noble consort, and encouraged by the loyalty and ability of his sons and daughter, the King went steadily on. During his severe illness in the winter of 1928-29 his people learnt, from one minister after another, of the life of ceaseless toil he had led for them ; and the heart of the world was won by the patience, fortitude and self-forgetfulness with which he bore his sufferings. As he recovered, he learned of the love that had watched over him at home and abroad. ' The realization of this,' he wrote to the nation from Craigwell House, ' has been among the most vivid experiences of my life,' and, he added, ' it was an encouragement beyond description to feel that my constant and earnest desire had been granted—the desire to gain the confidence and affection of my People. My thoughts have carried me even further than this. I cannot dwell upon the generous sympathy shewn to me by unknown friends in many other countries without a new and moving hope. I long to believe it possible that experiences such as mine may soon appear no longer exceptional, when the national anxieties of all the Peoples of the World shall be felt as a common source of human sympathy and a common claim on human friendship.'

Of what followed, there is no need to write. Those last years, and especially the last year of all, are burnt into our hearts, their memory unforgettable. Through patience, fortitude and ceaseless toil, sweetened constantly by

> That best part of a good man's life,
> His little, nameless, unremembered acts
> of kindness and of love

King George gained what Henry Drummond has rightly called the supreme good, the power to love ; to love so deeply, so truly, so selflessly and so universally, that the peoples of a world-wide empire felt him as a personal friend, and the nations acknowledged the great benefit of his influence. He became, in his own words, the head of this vast family. Shortly after he passed away, a little boy was found in a corner weeping. He was asked why he was weeping, for he had not wept when others had passed away. 'Ah,' he said through his tears, ' but I *knew* the King.'

And now it is our great privilege to hold the memory of that ' Last Audience.' There, in the heart of the Empire, were united the symbols of earthly majesty and of human love. No mark of dreariness, no hopeless black was there, but the glory of the Royal Standard, the Robes and the Insignia, and, resting among them, the fragrant wreath which marked a wife's unfailing love. Rising above these, and hallowing them with its solemn majesty, rose the Cross of

THE GLORY AND THE MAJESTY

the Redeemer, the Cross which, in loneliness and watchings, and in sufferings bravely borne, King George V had been privileged in some degree to share ; and far above all rose the four great candles which symbolize Eternal Life. At the memory of this scene we bow in speechless gratitude before that infinite Wisdom and Love which gave us such a King in such an hour ; and our heart echoes the words of David, ' Thine, O Lord, is the greatness, and the power, and the glory, and the victory, and the majesty.'

KING EDWARD VIII AS PRINCE

A MAN'S success in life is never an accident. He makes and takes his own opportunities. And his ability to make and take them is often decided in childhood and youth, by the qualities unconsciously imbibed at home and at school, and ripened by earnest effort.

The undoubted success of King Edward VIII, as Prince of Wales, was no exception to this rule ; nor was it an exception to the rule that disadvantages can be overcome. History shows that it is not a help but a hindrance to a young man to be Prince of Wales. To be always in the public eye, to have no choice as to one's career, to be largely denied the frank friendship and honest competition which make youth a joy—these are severe handicaps for a young man.

King Edward overcame these handicaps. He learnt to mix freely with rich and poor on a basis of true comradeship. He commanded respectful attention from the most varied audiences when he spoke on the problems of the day. As Master of the Merchant Navy and Fishing Fleet he watched over the interests of mariners. He was an efficient Naval and Army Officer. His farms in England and Canada are a benefit to agriculture. The business men of Britain acknowledge the high value of his services to commerce. At the Front and on his exacting journeys

'HIS HAPPIEST MOMENTS'

KING EDWARD VIII AS PRINCE

he won the trust and affection of the far-flung peoples of the British Commonwealth and America. He became known as one of the best landlords in England by the minute personal attention given to his large estates in town and country. He has done much to dissolve class and race antagonism. And his happiest moments were often spent among boys, at a boys' club, school or Scout Camp, or at an Unemployed Occupation Centre.

Why did King Edward succeed where many of his forerunners achieved so little ? First and foremost because of the wisdom and foresight of his parents. Neither the late King George V nor Queen Mary had been in the immediate succession to the Throne in their youth ; they had both known something of the ordinary difficulties of human life, and they had both gained through earnest effort a deep insight into the problems of simple people. They realized the value, to a young man, of having to make his own way, and they foresaw that in this century the Royal Family would be drawn into a far more intimate relationship to the people than had been possible before. While it was necessary for David, as he was known at home, to learn the special duties of a Prince, they determined that he should have his full chance to be a normal Englishman.

As a naval cadet he had to meet all the strenuous demands of Osborne and Dartmouth, and from time to time to face exacting public ceremonies, such as the Coronation, his instalment as Knight of the

Garter, and his investiture as Prince of Wales at Caernarvon Castle. He felt the severity of the effort, and it was with real joy that he flung himself into the life of a midshipman on a great battleship. Here at last he could really be his own age.

He longed to follow his father's career as a naval officer ; but part of his training was the constant putting aside of his own desires, and after three months at sea, during which he showed himself as smart and keen a middy as the Navy can produce, he had to return to his education ashore.

Like his grandfather, the young Prince was to go to Oxford, but under totally different circumstances. Instead of living apart, he was to occupy rooms in College and be an ordinary undergraduate. A year was spent in preparation for the University, part of it in France. Besides improving his French and his knowledge of France, he came to value the warm and genial atmosphere of a French home, and there is no doubt that France made a real contribution to his character. The young Englishman is too restrained, too afraid of showing feeling ; in France the Prince found encouragement for his own native gift for spontaneous friendliness. In consequence, he learnt to fit in to the life of Oxford in a way he could hardly have done had he come straight from the Navy.

Oxford introduced him to his fellow Englishmen on a wide scale. It made him part of the English scene, not as a Prince but as an individual. He entered fully and freely into the work, games and fun of under-

KING EDWARD VIII AS PRINCE

graduate life. Under the guidance of Professor Fiedler he also came to know many aspects of German life. When the World War suddenly interrupted his studies he acted as every other young man of mettle acted. He pressed his claims to immediate service at sea or abroad. But here his handicap was severe, for the authorities refused to risk such a precious life.

Up to this point he had been following the course mapped out by his parents ; now he asserted himself : he began to carve out the career which has set a new standard for Royalty, and made him the natural leader of the nation. By sheer persistence he asserted his right to serve overseas as an officer in the Guards, only to find that he had been allotted to the Staff of the Commander-in-Chief. Determined to be in the danger-zone, he became known as ' Dynamite Wales ' because of his constant tendency to ' go off.' By the end of the war he had rendered distinguished service in France, and seen the Italian and Egyptian fronts. Most important, he had shared the hardships of men from every part of the Empire, and come to know and admire them. Thus he laid the foundations for that remarkable capacity for world-wide friendship which has distinguished his career.

Through his war service, as he himself said, he found his manhood. He went to France a youth, and returned a man, to play an active part in caring for the disabled, in managing his estates, in cementing the bonds of Empire, in promoting foreign trade, in encouraging international friendship and reconciliation with Germany, in stimulating every kind of work on behalf of youth and of the unemployed. At times of especial trial, such as the winter of 1928–9 and again in that of 1931, his keen insight and tireless devotion have made him a leader in relieving distress, and in quickening new hope and courage. As the *Southern Daily Echo* said of him in 1929, ' The Prince does not do these things merely from a sense of duty. He acts on the promptings of his heart. That is why, wherever he goes where there is suffering he is able to leave some healing, helpful influence behind.' ' Helping others,' he once wrote in a personal letter, ' there's no better thing in life, when you come to analyse it.' Nor can these lines end more fitly than in the noble words of *The Times* on the eve of the new King's first broadcast to his Empire :

' In a world where force is being upheld as a principle of action the King has upheld the principle of kindness ; in a world divided by enmities he has drawn us together by his example of friendliness ; in a world weakened by fear he has asserted the confidence of hope. Many intolerable burdens remain to be lightened, but going forward in this Royal spirit we can say with the Shepherds of the Delectable Mountains, " This is a comfortable company ; you are welcome to us, for we have for the feeble as well as for the strong ; our Prince has an eye for what is done for the least of these ! " '

INDUSTRY

JOSIAH WEDGWOOD, THE QUEEN'S POTTER

JOSIAH Wedgwood was one of the greatest Englishmen of the eighteenth century. 'I call him the great Wedgwood,' said Gladstone. ' In my opinion, and I have considered the matter as well as I can, Wedgwood was the greatest man who ever, in any age, or in any country—I do not except, as far as our knowledge goes, any age or any country—applied himself to the important work of uniting art with industry.'

From childhood Wedgwood shewed the most delicate skill in moulding clay, but at seventeen, lameness prevented his continuing work at the potter's wheel ; and this, to quote Gladstone again, ' sent his mind inwards ; it drove him to meditate upon the laws and secrets of his art. The result was, that he arrived at a perception and grasp of them which might, perhaps, have been envied, certainly not have been owned, by an Athenian potter. Wedgwood completely revolutionized the character of the fabrics made in England at the period. He recalled into existence the spirit of Greek Art.'

This is high praise from a fellow-countryman ; yet more remarkable are the words of the German romantic writer, Novalis, who says that Goethe, the greatest genius of Germany, ' imparts to his works the very

INDUSTRY

qualities which the Englishman expresses in his wares ; the utmost simplicity, accuracy, suitability and permanence. He has done for German literature just what Wedgwood has accomplished in the sphere of English art.' In the words which Wedgwood's family inscribed on his monument, he 'converted a rude and inconsiderable Manufactory into an elegant Art and an important part of National Commerce.'

What were the qualities which enabled this man, who had left school at nine to follow his family's calling, to change for the better the artistic taste of a nation : to turn a lonely moorland settlement, approached only by rough tracks, into the centre of a great industry served by fine canals and roads : to make English pottery, as yet only used for the roughest domestic purposes in England, eagerly sought after by the cultured and titled from Moscow to the Mississippi : and to become the personal friend of the most eminent scientists and engineers of his day, a Fellow of the Royal Society and the Society of Antiquaries ?

Josiah Wedgwood was a born artist, with an exquisite perception of colour and form ; he was also a tireless thinker, ceaselessly engaged in scientific research. His creative powers are said to have been kindled by his affection for his little cousin Sarah, who was the first to believe in him, and who later, as his wife, shared his every plan and his every triumph. Selfishness had no place in his nature, and he worked less for personal gain than for the uplift of his art.

The nobility and purity of his character, the breadth

of his mind, the delicacy of his sympathy, the warmth of his interest in all that concerned the well-being of those around him, and his deep religious feeling gave to Wedgwood's art a quality which mere ability could not bestow, and rallied to his aid the rarest minds and the ablest co-workers. The nobility delighted to send the finest pieces from their collections for him to study; the Queen gave her name to his table-ware; the best sculptors of the century gathered at his works to cut the delicate models for his exquisite medallions and bas-reliefs; while Thomas Bentley, one of the most courtly and cultured Englishmen of the day, took charge of his London showrooms and made them a centre of society.

Wedgwood's early years were full of lonely toil, of long days spent in struggling with crude workmen, of long evenings spent in chemical research, of sleepless nights of thought, of weary weeks during which experiment after experiment was thwarted. Happiness came with Bentley's friendship and his own marriage; and then his powers were thrown into the wider work of developing roads through the Potteries, of fighting a Parliamentary campaign for the right to join the Trent and the Mersey by a canal, and of helping to raise the intellectual and moral level of the district by founding chapels and schools.

Wedgwood's earlier efforts as a potter were devoted to the search for new materials in which domestic pottery of artistic quality and moderate cost could be brought into the homes of the many. Once his fame

INDUSTRY

and fortune were established, he turned his attention to pure art. He discovered a black basalt in which vases and statues rivalling Etruscan ware were moulded, and a delicate jasper, used for bas-reliefs in white on a rich background of mazzarin blue. The portrait medallions and the ornamental vases and plaques wrought in this ware were a unique contribution to ceramic art, and though the designs on them reveal Wedgwood's indebtedness to Greek and Italian sculpture, they are yet strikingly original. But Wedgwood was even greater than his art, which was the overflow of a generous spirit. The long years of lonely research and experiment during which he was so often baffled by weakness and pain, by unprogressive workmen and by jealous competitors, did not sour his spirit; instead, they but prepared it to profit by the rare friendship of Bentley and the warm comradeship of his wife and children. It is in his *Letters*, collected and edited by Lady Farrar, that we see the real Wedgwood. They begin abruptly with the first letter to Bentley, to whom he was introduced by his physician while lying injured at Liverpool. The acquaintance quickly ripened into friendship, and during the long days of convalescence the two men exchanged the thoughts of a life-time on education, philosophy, literature and religion. Like Goethe and Schiller at Jena, they met never to part; the friendship of the struggling potter with his travelled and cultured partner had its parallel in that great friendship which produced the supreme works of German literature.

JOSIAH WEDGWOOD

Bentley became first Wedgwood's agent and then his partner. He had precisely the qualities needed to supplement those of his more original friend. Throughout their letters to each other there reigns an ever-increasing joy in the beauty of their companionship. No difference of opinion in business or art ever clouded their affection. To Wedgwood, Bentley's letters were lovely, a source of inspiration, a challenge to the highest achievement. 'The very feel of them, even before the seal is broken, cheers my heart and does me good, . . .' he writes. 'They inspire me with taste, emulation, and everything that is necessary for the production of fine things . . . I give you leave, my dear friend, to find fault with me as fast as you please.—The more and the oftener the better.'

The results of this constant inspiration were soon felt throughout Europe. The continent awoke to the fact that a new artistic influence was abroad. The great porcelain works at Sèvres and Dresden and Copenhagen no longer retained their easy supremacy. Thousands of skilled workmen were gathered in North Staffordshire, where twenty years before a few hundreds had carried on a crude and traditional craft. Tasteful china was replacing pewter and wood in the homes of the middle-classes. Till then the English nobility had used only porcelain from abroad, but now even royalty was ordering Wedgwood's services both at home and abroad.

Thus arose a great question—should Wedgwood and Bentley protect their discoveries and work for their own aggrandisement, or should they give all for the elevation of their craft ? The course chosen was the nobler one ; and its results in artistic stimulus and also in commercial prosperity were beyond all expectation. ' So far from being afraid of other people getting out patterns,' writes Wedgwood to his partner, ' we should glory in it. Throw out all hints we can and if possible have all the Artists in Europe working after our models. This w'd be noble and w'd suit both our dispositions and sentiments much better than all narrow, mercenary and selfish channels—the coats of mail which we are forging for our reluctant hearts, to case and hamper them in our journey through life, and prevent all benevolent overflowings for the good of their fellow-citizens. . . . There is nothing relating to business I so much wish for as being released from these degrading slavish chains, these mean and selfish fears of other people copying my works. . . I have always wanted to be released from it.'

Often the letters dwell on his delight in his home. ' Mrs. Wedgwood and the Wedgwoodikin ' are rarely absent from the earlier letters ; later ' the Wedgwoodikin ' multiplied into ' The Infantry,' and as the boys and girls developed they had a large place in their father's thought. Whatever the pressure of business, he would rise early in the morning and go riding with his sons, or if it was wet pursue studies and experiments with them ; over their education and that of his daughters he watched with lively care. One of his daughters became the mother of Charles Darwin, and the world of science owes a great debt to Wedgwood's insistence on liberal education for his girls as well as his boys. With his wife he discussed his every experiment. As a child she had encouraged him by her warm admiration. 'Don't you know, Josiah,' she is said to have exclaimed when as a lad he was down-hearted, 'that your eyes are so beautiful and so full of dreams that people like to look at you ? . . . You are going to be a great man some day.' No wonder he could write in manhood : ' I speak from experience in Female taste without which I should have made a poor figure among the Potts, not one of which of any consequence is finished without the approbation of my Sally.'

Wealth and fame came to Josiah Wedgwood, but he remained the same man. To his less fortunate relatives, and to all whom he employed he was a loyal friend. He was the first great employee of labour to provide good houses and educational facilities for his work-people. In public affairs he maintained the cause of liberty at home and abroad. He strongly opposed the war with the American Colonies ; he rejoiced at the fall of the Bastille ; and with his sons gave liberally to the cause of Polish patriotism. Clarkson's campaign against the slave trade was largely financed by him, and the firm struck a jasper medallion shewing a negro slave kneeling, with the inscription 'Am I not a man and a brother ? ' In private and in public he lived to the full the simple Christianity which he professed, and brightened the dreary wastes of mortal existence by the radiance of his rare affection.

SIR ALFRED YARROW

ON a windy Sunday morning in mid-August, 1878, the British Fleet lay at anchor off Portsmouth in readiness for a royal Review. Church Service was over. The bands were playing that amusing song from *H.M.S. Pinafore* which referred to Mr. W. H. Smith, who, as First Lord of the Admiralty, was with the Fleet, when two remarkable little vessels were seen approaching from the East at a great speed. Under a hundred feet long, with two funnels abreast amidships, those little steel craft dashed through the rough waters at 20 knots an hour, their light hulls bending considerably under the strain of being alternatively supported on a wave amidships and on waves at bow and stern. On the deck of one boat were discernible a handsome man of thirty-six or so, accompanied by a lady.

The battleships' crews greeted the newcomers with great enthusiasm. They realized the daring nature of the voyage which had been undertaken from the Thames to Portsmouth in rough weather with such light craft ; and the more experienced naval officers must have realized that this voyage was to open a new chapter in naval history. The little boats, which had already been the subject of acrimonious debate in Parliament, were the first torpedo-boats to navigate in open waters, and their speed was unprecedented.

SIR ALFRED YARROW

The gentleman and the lady on board were Mr. and Mrs. Alfred Yarrow, who, realizing the perilous nature of the voyage, had not cared to expose their crews to dangers they themselves did not face. It was by no means certain that the hulls would stand the strain of the rough water, and at one point in the voyage Yarrow had advised the pilot to leave the centre of the boat and go to bow or stern, because if the vessel broke it would occur just where he was sitting, and it would be uncomfortable for him to find part of his body in one end of the the ship and part in the other. However, nothing more serious than a good wetting was encountered, and on August 14th the two vessels escorted Queen Victoria from Cowes to Portsmouth, one on either side of the Royal Yacht—a breach of etiquette which was gladly forgiven by Her Majesty, who sent that evening a special message to Yarrow, through the Admiral of the Fleet, that nothing in the Review had interested her so much as these vessels. A few days later King Edward VII, then Prince of Wales, made a trip in one of the boats, under Alfred Yarrow's personal supervision, and thoroughly enjoyed the great speed of the run. It is worth recording that King Edward and the young engineer had been contemporary and eager attendants at Professor Faraday's lectures on electricity.

From that time the torpedo boat, which was already being employed by Russia and the Argentine, became a regular feature of the Royal Navy. The first boats were designed to ram the enemy with a torpedo on

INDUSTRY

the end of a long spar, and escape under cover of the explosion ; the introduction of the Whitehead self-propelling torpedo led to the launching of torpedoes over the side or from tubes, and one of these early torpedo boats, built by Yarrow, was placed in charge of King George V, then Prince George. She was the first boat fitted with triple expansion engines and attained the then unprecedented speed of 22.4 knots.

In 1892 Alfred Yarrow called on Admiral Sir John Fisher at the Admiralty and informed him that he had seen exceptionally fast torpedo-boats being built in French dockyards, boats which would surpass all our own in performance. Sir John asked him to make a full report, and to submit proposals for a boat to surpass the French vessels. The result was the building of the first Destroyers, *H.M.S. Havock* and *H.M.S. Hornet.* They were 180 feet long and the *Hornet* attained a speed of 27.3 knots. The Admiralty promptly ordered a large number of destroyers. Many of these were built in other yards from Yarrow's designs, which were communicated to the builders by the Admiralty, an act which caused Yarrow great annoyance until the Secretary of the Navy publicly acknowledged his firm as the originators of this new class of ship.

From this time on Alfred Yarrow became known throughout the world as designer and builder of Torpedo Boat Destroyers of the front rank. His vessels rendered notable service in the Russo-Japanese War and in the Great War. The high speeds attained by destroyers re-acted on merchant shipping, and led to the fast services of to-day. In the achievement of these speeds three men played a leading role—M. Normand of Havre, Thorneycroft, and Alfred Yarrow.

No one could have been more unlike the conventional conception of an armament manufacturer than this Londoner whose ships were plying not only the Seven Seas, but the rivers and lakes of the world. From childhood he had been distinguished by two traits, ' a talent for engineering and a passionate thirst for affection—to give and to receive.' The words are those of his first schoolmaster. Alfred Yarrow was ' a mother's boy ' ; he always spoke highly of his father's deep kindness and high sense of honour, but his mother remained his intimate friend and counsellor till she passed away at the age of ninety. Esther Lindo, as she had been before her marriage to Edgar Yarrow, was a beautiful, warm-hearted and highly gifted woman, a close relative and intimate acquaintance of Lord Beaconsfield ; her family could trace its descent from King David, and Alfred Yarrow was always proud of his semi-Jewish descent, though his mother had become a Christian and brought him up in the Nonconformist faith. When her son, after leaving University College School and completing his apprenticeship to a London firm of marine engineers, started his own small engineering shop, she followed his every move, accompanied him on business journeys, and watched with eagle eye over his interests. When

INDUSTRY

a large general dealer and sugar refiner refused to pay bills for repairs to his machinery, she ordered large quantities of household supplies from him, and in reply to their invoice forwarded her son's account. During his honeymoon, she detected a fraud which was being perpetrated in his absence, and wired him to return, enabling him to counter his opponent's move. It is a question whether Yarrow would have won through his early years of depressing struggle but for her constant support.

These early struggles had nothing to do with ship building. From childhood Yarrow had given evidence of remarkable inventive powers, and his early efforts had sometimes been embarrassing to the household ; on one occasion he nearly electrocuted the cook, and on another he put out the gas in all the neighbouring houses ; but he also constructed the first overhead telegraph in London, and produced a very workable marmalade slicer. His first commercial proposition was the Yarrow-Hilditch steam-plough, which was followed by the Yarrow-Hilditch steam-carriage : the first went too slowly commercially, and the second too fast politically—the net result of its journeys was an Act of Parliament necessitating the carriage of a red flag before any mechanically propelled vehicle on the road, an Act which prevented the development of the motor-car in England until its repeal in 1897, and produced the amusing result that a steam-roller always had a navvy with a flag doing the slow march before it. Yarrow did some work as Consulting Engineer, but he suffered too intensely under the suspicion that bribes were being offered him; and he dropped repairing ships' engines because he could only get work by retiring to a bar with the mate. Those were not promising beginnings for an armament manufacturer, nor were two years of miscellaneous engineering in some old buildings on the Isle of Dogs, during the second of which he and his partner lost £2,000.

It was at this point that Yarrow bethought himself of happy days spent on the Thames with his friend Hilditch, in a little steam launch of their own construction. The *Isis* had been a great source of joy; she was to become a still greater source of progress.

'Yarrow & Hedley' advertised as builders of steam launches. Within three days the fairy king appeared in the form of an old gentleman, a Colonel Halpin, who ordered a 24-foot steam launch at £145. She cost £200 to build; but she created a sensation. At the end of the season Yarrow bought her back for £100 and sold her the same day for £200. The next year he again repurchased at £100 and sold her to a Russian nobleman for £300. She went to Petrograd, and started Yarrow's reputation overseas. Very soon Yarrow & Hedley were building steam launches for customers in all parts of the world. They achieved high speeds in their boats, and, having no serious competitors, they were able to command good prices. It was this reputation as launch builders which brought the first order for torpedo-boats from the Argentine Government, followed quickly by orders from Russia,

INDUSTRY

Holland, France, Greece, Spain, Austria, Italy and China. The two Torpedo Boats which made such a sensation in the 1878 Review had been ordered for Russia, but taken over by our Admiralty owing to the international tension in the Near East. Financial troubles were now over, and Alfred Yarrow could devote himself to the endless research and experiment which contributed so considerably to a universal increase of speed at sea.

One afternoon in 1875 Yarrow was hurrying to work, when he saw two gentlemen standing on the bridge which leads to the Isle of Dogs. Impressed with their appearance, he stopped and asked if he could be of any service. He quietly divined that they had been to his works and been turned away by his partner. Captain Young, R.N., and his companion had, in fact, come on behalf of the Nyassa Mission, to ask if the firm could build a light steamer of shallow draught, which could be disconnected and carried across country by native bearers in pieces of not more than 50 lbs. weight. The steamer was to navigate the Zambesi river up to Lake Nyassa, 'the Lake of Storms,' where she was to assist in subduing the slave trade.

The *Ilala* was built in ten weeks, and proved thoroughly satisfactory ; later the firm built the gunboats *Pioneer* and *Adventure* for the Admiralty, which were also sent in pieces to Lake Nyassa. The result was the total suppression of the Slave Trade on the Lake. These boats were followed by others built for

THE FIRST MOTOR TORPEDO BOAT, COWES, 1906

various parts of the world where boats had to be dismantled and carried at certain parts of the journey. Such Yarrow-built boats played a large part in Stanley's expedition to the Congo and in the attempted relief of Khartoum ; if the Government had listened to Alfred Yarrow's urgent protestations for the rapid building of a river-fleet there is little doubt that Gordon and his force would have been rescued in time. The final development of this experience in solving the especial problems of river navigation was the building of the gunboats which played such a vital part in General Townsend's first advance and General Maude's final victory in Mesopotamia.

Yarrow was quick to see the possibilities of the motor boat, and during the Cowes week of 1906 a motor launch built by him created considerable interest. Lord Fisher wired to Yarrow that His Majesty the King wished to see some manoeuvres by the boat, and the next day her builder brought her alongside the *Victoria and Albert* and took the Royal party for a short trip. The King wished to travel at her highest possible speed, but Queen Alexandra put in quickly : " No, not whilst the King is on board. Do not run the slightest risk. I will go again later." His Majesty and some of the party then left the boat, but the Queen stayed on board and had a trip at a speed unprecedented for such a small vessel.

It has only been possible, in such a short space, to state briefly the results of Yarrow's work. These results were obtained by combining his inventiveness and his innate love of his fellows in a life of ceaseless but joyous work. The two qualities constantly interacted, for while Yarrow's love of engineering drove him constantly along paths leading to higher speed in ships, his love for his fellow-men made him equally concerned for the safety and comfort of the crew. The early advances in speed were achieved by using forced draught under tubular boilers; in the great heats developed, tubes frequently burst, and stokers were scalded to death. A Russian captain who had secured from the firm plans and models for building a hundred torpedo boats returned some time later with a pure white head of hair, and in reply to Yarrow's startled look, told him that every white hair was a burst boiler tube. The solution of this problem preyed on Yarrow's mind, and it is profoundly interesting, considering his Jewish ancestry, that the solution was finally revealed to him in a dream. He awoke, made a sketch of the plan revealed, and went to sleep again; the next day he telegraphed to the Russian Government that a device had been discovered to safeguard the stokers. It worked perfectly, and marked a great step forward in marine engineering.

There was a second channel through which Yarrow's affectionate nature operated to forward his progress, and that was through his relations with his staff. Though he was a sound economist, and never indulged in weak generosity, Yarrow cared deeply for his employees, and had little trouble with strikes. At the time of the great Engineers' Strike in 1897 his men struck in sympathy with their Unions, but many went into his office to bid him farewell, some even with tears in their eyes. He was able to keep his works going in a unique manner. He advertised for non-union labour, and quartered the applicants on the Royal Mail Steamer *Southampton*, which he bought and moored opposite the works. Everything possible was done for the men's comfort, and launches took them ashore and met them again in such a way that they were never molested by picketers. Yarrow's whole attitude during the strike did much to mitigate ill-feeling, and had a considerable effect on public opinion.

Early in the strike Yarrow had the satisfaction of conveying King George V and Queen Mary, then Duke and Duchess of York, from Westminster to the India Docks in one of his small torpedo boats. The men refused to drive the engines, but gentlemen from the technical staff took their places and successfully conducted the trip. Yarrow's success in dealing with labour problems also brought H.M. the King of the Belgians to the works for an afternoon of consultation and discussion.

With his immediate staff the now famous engineer kept on close terms of intimacy, and the most famous of his inventions, the Yarrow Marine Boiler, had its origin in a lunch-time chat with William Crush, then head of the boiler department. Up to that time tubular boilers had been made with bent tubes, which made efficient cleaning almost impossible. After many experiments Yarrow decided on straight tubes, so arranged that each one could be examined and cleaned with ease. So thorough was the preliminary examination of difficulties that ten years elapsed before such a boiler was placed in a destroyer, and little alteration has been found necessary since that time.

As previously mentioned, Alfred Yarrow had been an eager student of Professor Faraday as a young man, and his success as a marine engineer was largely due to the application of the principles of scientific research to the problems of ship-building. The great Experimental Tank at the National Physical Laboratory, Teddington, came into being through his energy and generosity. Before it was opened in 1911 all experimental trials had to be conducted abroad. Yarrow was determined that the country should not suffer this disadvantage any longer, and as no help could be obtained from the Government, he offered £20,000 to the Royal Society on condition that a similar sum be raised for maintenance for ten years. Later he presented the Royal Society with £100,000, which is used to support three Yarrow Research Professorships, and made large gifts to Girton College and the British Association for similar purposes. It will thus be seen that Sir Alfred Yarrow and Josiah Wedgwood were alike in their devotion to scientific research, despite the wholly different nature of their productions ; they were also alike in their generous and affectionate, yet thoroughly practical, manner of conducting a great business.

SIR ALFRED YARROW

As the firm grew, it was found that the Thames was no longer the best spot for the work, and after exhaustive search it was decided to move to Scotstoun on the Clyde. The move was accomplished without any cessation of work ; shipbuilding was started on the Clyde within a few months of the first sod being cut, and the Poplar Works constructed machinery up to the last moment. The Scotsman who makes his way in London is a byword ; the Londoner who succeeds in Scotland is a rarity, but the name Yarrow has become so associated with the Clyde that many people believe the firm to be a Scotch one.

The first destroyer was launched at Scotstoun on July 14th, 1908. Five years later Yarrow, now seventy-two years of age, left Scotland and made his home in Surrey, with the purpose of devoting himself to the many and varied interests which he had acquired. He was to keep in touch with the firm by daily telephonic conversation, exchange of visits and correspondence, but the details of the yard were to be controlled by the younger members of the firm, among whom were his sons Harold, Norman and Eric. Ten months after his retirement War was declared, and at 4 a.m. on August 5 the order came through from Yarrow to accelerate the work on three destroyers. Next day he gave orders at his own risk for two more destroyers to be built. He returned to the yard, and threw all the power of his personality into the work. Before the Armistice was signed twenty-nine destroyers had left the yard, and speeds of nearly 40 knots had been attained. The fleet of gunboats for the Tigris had been built. A book could be written of the exploits of Yarrow-built boats, every one of which proved a success in action ; and much could be written of Alfred Yarrow's personal interest in the crews of each. Through the insistence of Lord Fisher and Admiral Jellicoe he was made a baronet in 1916 ; to Fisher he was 'my beloved Yarrow,' and Lord Jellicoe wrote from *H.M.S. Iron Duke* : ' I have reported officially that the sooner you *design* and build many more T.B.D.'s the better for the country.'

This was surely enough for a man of over seventy : but Yarrow's genius was at its most fertile during the war years. There was about it an element which can only be described as motherliness—a swift perception of human needs and a tireless resource in meeting them. He designed protective veils for snipers, and a method for protection against trench-feet, and another for defence against fleas and mosquitos. He started a special department for the manufacture of artificial limbs, and was one of the first to realize the need for adequate propaganda abroad in the neutral press. He carried on this propaganda at his own expense until stopped by Foreign Office, upon which he personally laid the whole matter before the King. As a ship-builder he was especially concerned for safety at sea. He designed an excellent life-saving waistcoat, eighty of which were given to each destroyer launched by the firm, and brought forward a method for protecting merchant ships from submarines

SIR ALFRED YARROW

by a diversion of their smoke. He also offered large sums to be given as rewards for the first detection and for the destruction of submarines by merchantmen.

Sir Alfred's last thirteen years were peaceful and happy ones. He made very considerable gifts to the Royal Society, the British Association and Girton College for the promotion of research, and interested himself in a large number of constructive charities, all designed to help the deserving help themselves. I had the privilege of considerable correspondence with him in 1931, and was greatly impressed with his ready helpfulness and his keen interest in every aspect of life. At that time he often stayed at the Savoy Hotel, and his great delight was to have tea in an aeroplane circling over London. He passed away on the 24th January, 1932, after a life of amazing energy, a man whom success had never spoiled and who retained to the last the beautiful qualities of his childhood.

SHAPERS OF MEN

EDWARD BOWEN AND THE HARROW SONGS

EDWARD Ernest Bowen, brother of Lord Bowen, came of a Protestant Irish family from County Mayo, Connaught. His father, the Rev. Christopher Bowen, was curate at Woolaston near Chepstow when Edward was born, and both the brothers received their early education at the Rev. Selwyn's School, Blackheath. The family had now moved to London, where the father became perpetual curate of St. Mary Magdalene, Southwark. The elder brother left Blackheath for Rugby. Edward continued his education at King's College, London, before going to Trinity, Cambridge, where he had a brilliant career. The one disappointment of his life was that he missed being Senior Classic, but he was placed fourth in the First Class, and elected to a Fellowship at Trinity.

Bowen had been reared in an atmosphere of strict evangelical piety. Like his famous brother, he was gifted with a rare sense of humour; and, as became apparent at Harrow, he was a poet of no mean order. These gifts apparently came to him through his mother, the daughter of Sir Richard and Lady Steele, and the grand-daughter of Count d'Alton. As his individuality developed, he thought his way far beyond the Evangelical position, but he retained a deep sympathy with his parents, and was throughout his life a most devoted son, especially to his mother, who outlived him.

After one term at Marlborough he went as an assistant master to Harrow and held the post till his passing, forty-two years later. At one time he thought of entering Parliament; but his defeat by Arthur Balfour in the Hertford constituency in 1880 finally decided him against a political career, and he finished his life as a Harrow master.

In the scholastic profession he was known as a bold but practical reformer, whose views were eagerly sought by educators throughout the country and from abroad. 'Punishments, rewards and marks,' he regarded as the three great drawbacks to education, and declared that 'Boys ought hardly ever to be punished against their will.' Nevertheless, he was a strong disciplinarian with his own quaint but effective methods. His wider fame rests on the poems of school life which he wrote primarily for Harrow.

There is no question that the noble series of songs which Bowen and Farmer produced for Harrow are the expression of a vision, and one of the means of its fulfilment. The songs were struck off in intervals from intense toil—toil which always had one motive, to make boy-life free, happy and inspiring. In the words of Dr. H. M. Butler, Bowen's headmaster and true friend, 'The songs proved from the first, and never lost their spell, of quite extraordinary value in promoting good fellowship among the boys and in forging links of love and loyalty between passing generations of Harrow men.'

Tennyson spoke highly of Edward Bowen's songs, and ' Forty Years On,' which is always sung standing at Harrow, has justly been called the grandest song in modern literature. It was not easily accepted at first, as the conjunction of the Divine name with such a subject as football seemed irreverent to orthodox thought, and had Matthew Arnold not been living at Byron House at the time it was written, the glorious challenge of the last verse might have been suppressed. The manuscript was taken to him, and he gave his unqualified approval to the great verse closing:

> God give us bases to guard and beleaguer,
>   Games to play out, whether earnest or fun ;
> Fights for the fearless, and goals for the eager,
>   Twenty, and thirty, and forty years on !

Thus Harrow owes her greatest song in part to a Rugbeian, who had himself written a great meditative lyric of school life, ' Rugby Chapel.'

The perfect unity of thought existing between Edward Bowen and John Farmer was never better illustrated than in the production of ' Forty Years On.' Farmer was just coming out of chapel when the MS. was handed to him. He glanced through it and exclaimed ' I suppose nobody has a piano in his pocket ? ' Nobody had, so adjournment was made to the nearest instrument, and in a very short time the stirring notes of the melody were ringing out for the first time. Farmer left Harrow when Dr. Butler resigned the Headmastership, and the sentiments of Edward Bowen at the ending of their long partnership are expressed in the exquisite lyric ' Songs.'

' Forty Years On ' and ' Willow The King ' are widely known. The exquisite delicacy of ' Fairies,' ' June and the Scholar,' and ' She Was a Shepherdess ' give Bowen a high place in modern lyric poetry. A deeper and more stirring note is struck in ' Raleigh ' and ' Byron Lay ' :

>   When Raleigh rose to fight the foes,
>   We sprang to work and will ;
>   When Glory gave to Drake the wave,
>   She gave to us the hill.
>   The ages drift in rolling tide,
>   But high shall float the morn
>   Adown the stream of England's pride,
>   When Drake and we were born !
>   For we began when he began,
>   Our times are one ;
>   His glory thus shall circle us
>   Till time be done.

So runs the first verse of ' Raleigh,' the later ones wedding Shakespeare's muse and Sidney's chivalry to the story of Harrow. ' Byron Lay ' tells humorously of Byron's laziness at school and Peel's tremendous industry, how the one exasperated the masters and the other the boys ; in the last verse the tone changes :

EDWARD BOWEN AND THE HARROW SONGS

>   Byron lay, solemnly lay,
>   Dying for freedom, far away ;
>   Peel stood up on the famous floor,
>   Ruled the people, and fed the poor ;
> None so narrow the range of Harrow ;
> Welcome poet and statesman too ;
>   Doer and dreamer, dreamer, dreamer,
>   Doer and dreamer, dream and do.

Bowen was too wise a teacher, and too young-hearted, to strike always this stirring note. Many of the songs are sheer Gilbertian nonsense, as the one in which John Lyon, the Founder of Harrow, goes to Queen Elizabeth to ask for a charter, as she sits with Drake 'watching the Tilbury guns at play,' and gets the answer :

>   And this is my charter, firm and free
>   This is my royal, great decree—
>   *Hits to the rail shall count for three,*
>   *And six when fairly over :*
>   And if anyone comes and makes a fuss
>   Send the radical off to us,
>   And I will tell him I choose it thus
>   And so will the bold sea-rover.

Edward Bowen was a man of exceptional gifts, of deep, unspoken spirituality and of rare beauty of character. Few men have given themselves so completely to boys ; few have been so beloved by pupils and colleagues, or become so widely respected throughout the profession. This love and respect did not come at once, for Bowen was too daringly himself, too original, and too exacting to be readily understood. He was one of the first men in England openly to accept the verdict of the Higher Criticism and to teach the Bible in the light of it ; his articles in the *National Review* on ' Bishop Colenso and the Pentateuch ' and ' The Recent Criticism of the Old Testament ' were a shock to the literalists, but they cleared the air in Britain and helped to open the way for broader thinking. Though of a military family, and gifted with exceptional insight into military history, he was strongly opposed to war. He incurred sharp hostility at first for his frank and open comradeship with boys. But he was a teacher who worked harder for his classes and got more work out of them than any man had done before, an achievement all the greater that he was set to develop the first ' Modern Side ' in one of the great Public Schools. To bring actuality into his history lessons he followed the campaigns of Germany in 1864 and 1870 on foot. He entered France with the German armies, and spent Christmas in Paris during the siege of the Commune. He visited almost every battlefield in Europe and brought away mementos which he would display in class with imaginative comments. Each evening he spent many hours preparing for the next day's classes, always determined to bring out some new and interesting point. He brought all the powers of a gifted intellect to bear on his lessons, and then transfused the whole with a delicious sense of fun—what other Public School master of that day kept tin soldiers in his desk, or offered as a prize for correct sentences 'a six-sided lead pencil bought of the grandson of the only publisher whom Napoleon the First shot?' This sense of sheer delight in teaching flashes out in such quaint humorous songs as 'Euclid,' in which all the difficulties of the fifth proposition are ascribed to the 'little black demon, who lives in the corner at C.'

Mr. Bowen was also an athlete of note, and the first Harrow master to identify himself with the games, into which he introduced many interesting features, being careful to leave the management strictly to the boys themselves ; he joined regularly in his boys' football up to his sixty-fifth year, and many of his songs cast the mantle of poetry round the daily struggles with bat and ball. He loved hardihood and simplicity, coupled with comradeship and consideration for others, and in nearly every song—even in the one about the little black demon at C—there is a kindly challenge to finer, hardier living.

The songs were written for community singing at school. During forty-two years twenty-eight came from his pen, and of these all but five were composed by John Farmer, who shared to the full his love of boyhood and his longing to see it strong and free. With deft fingers Edward Bowen has touched on all the common things of the school day and transfigured them. Football and cricket, the scholar and the athlete, the professional guesser and the sulker, Sober Dick the dreamer and Tom the doer, morning school and evening twilight, the quaint prejudices and dreams of boyhood, the school bell and the school's history—all make subjects for songs. Through each rings the voice of the great teacher, speaking to all generations of Harrovians and to many beyond the borders of Harrow those words of good cheer which he first uttered for his own pupils.

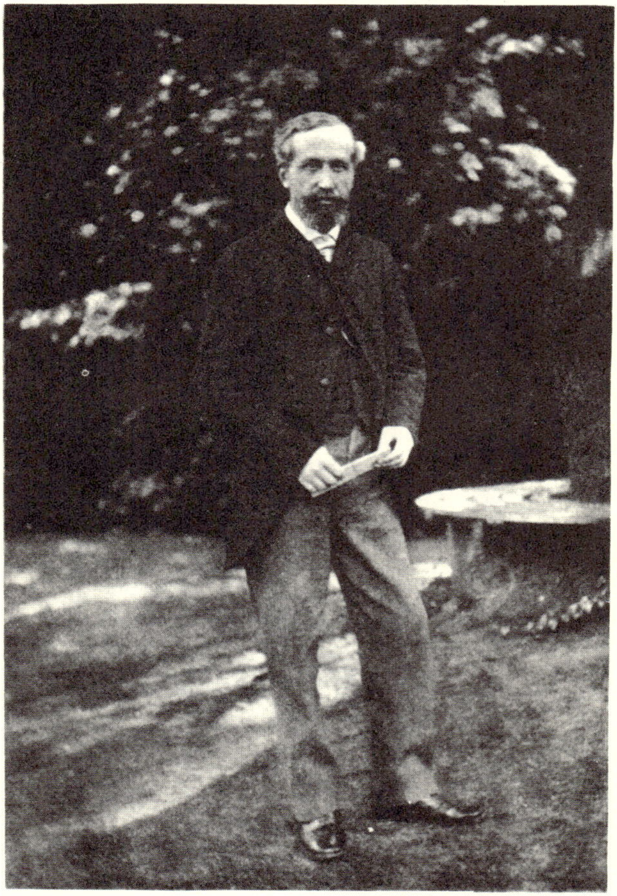

Yours very truly

E E Bowen

SIR JOHN McCLURE, LL.D., Mus.Doc.

SIR JOHN McCLURE OF MILL HILL

THE struggle between Roundhead and Cavalier did not cease with the close of the Civil War nor with the Restoration. The Act of Uniformity perpetuated that deep cleavage of thought, and split the English nation into two parties, the one of which had access to the Public Schools, the Universities, the Professions and the Services, while the other had to confine its energies to commerce and manufacture, the ministry or emigration. This was certainly to the benefit of the Colonies, especially of those which later became the United States of America, and also to commerce and industry at home; such families as those of Fry, Rowntree, Cadbury, Chivers, Hartley, Wedgwood and so on were all Dissenters who brought enlightenment and culture to bear upon great trading concerns. But the cleft between Church and Chapel was a wide one, with deep social and political implications which often caused each party to hate and despise the other only too cordially.

Two years after the battle of Trafalgar a group of London Dissenters—Baptist, Congregational, Presbyterian—banded together to found a school with a new outlook. Mill Hill School was at first known as ' The Protestant Dissenters' Grammar School ' but it was conceived in a broader spirit than its grim name seems to imply. Its purpose was to provide for the sons of

Nonconformists an education such as Eton or Harrow gave to those of Anglicans, but from the first the Founders proclaimed their unwillingness to exclude any boy on grounds of religion, and the promise has been nobly kept. One of the earliest boys became a Bishop, and the School is said to have sent out more Anglican clergymen than Nonconformist ministers. In 1907, when Nonconformists were still going to prison rather than pay for the upkeep of Church of England schools, the Headmaster of Mill Hill could say that more than half his staff and many of the boys were members of the ecclesiastical church, and, he added, 'The mass of Biblical truth on which all Protestant scholars are agreed is so vast, and the ignorance of boys is so great, that I have never yet had any leisure to turn my attention to any of the points of difference between the Church of England and Nonconformist Protestants.' That is a position widely accepted in schools during the last few years, but at the time of utterance it was almost hopelessly in advance of the general thought, even of that in many Public Schools.

By a singular felicity of choice the Founders had built the school on the summit of a long ridge from which one looks over the vale of Middlesex to Harrow and can, on a very clear day, discern the towers of Windsor Castle. Yet it took over a hundred years of work and the common agonies of the Great War to bridge the gulf between the schools on Harrow Hill and Mill Hill, or to bring a Royal visitor from the

Castle to the younger school. So much did it take to win for Nonconformists a just place in the national education. It was not one man's work, but the deep devotion of generations of Old Boys and supporters which brought the school through every shift of fortune, and found at last the man who was to come in its darkest hour and lead it out into the full tide of the national life.

That man was John David McClure, a shrewd, sturdy humorous Lancashire Scot, educated at Holly Mount, Wigan and Owens College, Manchester, his Northern toughness mellowed by subsequent years at Trinity, Cambridge, by nation-wide lecturing for the University Extension Movement, and by his union with Miss Marion Johnstone, the daughter of a Scottish Border family, to whom he paid such stirring tribute on one of the greatest occasions of his Headmastership.

John David McClure was a compound of many simples. He had all Arnold's deep religious earnestness, and was one of the very few men who have made school chapel a source of constant inspiration. He possessed Thring's ability to secure an appropriate setting for educational work of a high order. He shared Bowen's enthusiasm for games and his capacity to share the thoughts and feelings of a boy's life. And he was a scholar of wide attainments, a mathematician and an astronomer who became while Headmaster first a Doctor of Laws and then a Doctor of Music.

All these solid qualities were seasoned with a strong dash of Gilbert and Sullivan. There was a perpetual ripple of humour around McClure, and at times he would delight the School with nonsense verses or with orchestral compositions of perfect academic structure, built on melodies from the music halls, over which the professional musicians engaged to supplement the school orchestra would collapse in helpless laughter. The days too were full of music. McClure was the first man to make music a major subject carried on in regular school hours, and the choral singing in chapel was a revelation to boys who only knew the ill-assorted hymns of many Nonconformist chapels of that day. If he was one of the men who made Nonconformity respected in cultured circles, it was because he was a pioneer in a broader and more beautiful form of life and thought in his own religion. The liturgies which he drew up for the School chapel challenge comparison with those of any church or age, and thanks to him we became acquainted with many of the great hymns of the Church, some of which have since found their way into Nonconformist hymnals. The rich and mellow beauty of his own voice as he read the Scriptures or led the prayers was the expression of a generous and noble faith, and no one who saw him march from his stall to the pulpit, still singing with all his heart the last verse of the hymn, doubted that his worship of God was whole-hearted and radiantly joyous. His sermons were quiet, and appealed rather to the intellect than the emotions, but they were such that his boys were not afraid to discuss and ponder them ; more valued still were the friendly talks from the

Lectern on a Thursday morning, when, leaning upon the wings of the eagle, he would take us into his confidence and share with us the problems and the triumphs of his own spiritual life. There are limits to what can be done for a mixed crowd of boys in the matter of religion. Many of us may have come to no certain faith at school, for it is the privilege of a man to come to know God for himself and not through the words of another ; but one thing is certain, we all know that there was such a thing as faith, that it was a great and beautiful thing, and that it made life grand and happy. Those who were religiously inclined gained broader views and a deep sense of the value of beauty in worship ; much narrow Puritanism melted in the Mill Hill Chapel without loss in sincerity and power.

As the years lengthened and the school grew in numbers and in vision, there was added to the great natural beauty of Mill Hill the charm of buildings which it would be difficult to rival, all of which were the generous gifts of Old Boys. And even as lads we knew that there rested over the place another and yet greater beauty, the beauty of a strong character steadily growing in patience and tenderness and breadth of sympathy, and the beauty of a rare partnership between a noble man and a gracious lady, which brought a sweet breath of home into the strenuous life of the school. Sir John and Lady McClure (as they justly came to be) gave themselves utterly to Mill Hill, not for fame or reward, but because they saw that it embodied a great ideal of which England stood in need—the ideal, not of secular or unsectarian education, but of inter-denominational education, of the education of youth in a comradeship of religious faith, which could, in Tennyson's grand words,

> Let knowledge grow from more to more,
>   But more of reverence in us dwell,
> That mind and soul, according well,
>   May make one music as before
> But vaster . . . .

There may be many ways up a mountain, McClure was never tired of saying, but they all meet at the top, and though the views from different paths may be totally different, they will all be apparent at the summit.

Yet if it came to be said that McClure was Mill Hill and Mill Hill was McClure, this did not mean that he was alone in his vision, but rather that he embodied in himself the ideals for which a singularly devoted company of men were standing. Thanks to the marvellous loyalty of the Old Boys and the self-effacing service of the Staff, he was able to take an almost defeated school and make it one of the first in the land. It must not be imagined that the way was easy. The School was on the verge of collapse when a group of Old Boys, some of whom had known McClure at Cambridge, asked him to take the Headmastership. He was then reading for the Bar and acting as Professor of Astronomy at Queen's College, London. The offer had distinct possibilities. The School had had a period of prosperity under Dr.

Weymouth, the compiler of 'The Resultant Greek Testament' and 'The New Testament in Modern Speech.' Among his assistants had been Dr. (afterwards Sir James) Murray, who issued the first part of the New English Dictionary while at the School, the Rev. Robert Harley of Mathematical fame, and Dr. Frederick Stockton, whose arrival meant that two of the three D.Litt.s in existence were on the staff together. The older Universities had been opened to Nonconformists in Dr. Weymouth's first year, and during sixteen years his pupils gained twenty-six first classes in honours, including six first places, and six of them became Fellows of Colleges. Yet the trend of the School still ran steadily towards the University of London, no scholarships were available elsewhere, and only after fifteen years was a single Exhibition gained at Oxford. This obstinate clinging to London as the main outlet was a tradition which McClure had to reckon with.

It tended to mark the School out as one apart from the Public Schools, moving in an orbit of its own, and not even the visits of Thomas Hughes in 1873 and of Mr. Gladstone in 1879 had availed to bring national recognition to Mill Hill. It took McClure sixteen years of solid toil to achieve that—years in which he had to conquer the serious difficulties left by Weymouth's successor, to inspire the School and its supporters with new ideals, and to gain the confidence of the solid Nonconformist business men who formed the bulk of the parents, and who were imbued with a profound distrust of Oxford and Cambridge. Of this I speak with feeling, for I was one of those who profited directly ; I do not believe that any other man than McClure could have conquered my parents' distrust of the older Universities. It began to be said throughout Britain that if there was one man in the country who could be expected to make a boy a Christian, it was Dr. McClure of Mill Hill ; and to Mill Hill countless steady homes entrusted their sons in consequence. At the same time his attainments as a scholar and as a musician, and his high standing in the profession, attracted universal respect among the cultured and scholarly. The fortunate coincidence of the Centenary of the School with the presence in the House of seven Old Millhillians as supporters of the Campbell-Bannerman Government brought the Prime Minister as guest of honour to the Centenary celebrations, and this fact, coupled with the princely gifts of Old Boys, drew the general attention of Britain to Mill Hill. The decision of the Governors to depart from all precedent and permit military training in 1911, and the bearing of the new corps under Captain (now Major) N. G. B. James at the Royal Review in that year, opened a new era of co-operation with the older Public Schools.

McClure was not content with such a limited sense of success ; in his heart and mind there was going on an activity of love which made it impossible for him to think in terms lesser than the good of the nation. Truth is one, and the search for her in the nation's education must be one. The teaching profession was at that time hopelessly divided, not only by religious differences, but by classes and cliques. University, Public School, Secondary, Elementary and Technical teachers were at loggerheads, or affected to ignore each other's existence ; and the efforts of the more far-seeing to make teaching into an organized profession with a common council were perpetually wrecked on the shoals of class prejudice. It was the task of McClure to bring all these warring elements into harmony, and after that to persuade the Government to acknowledge the achievement. The Royal Society of Teachers, as it is called to-day, had its rise in his tireless work of reconciliation among the varied bodies representing the profession. The knighthood which followed was a well-deserved one.

Amid all this strenuous work outside Mill Hill McClure continued to teach more hours in class than do most headmasters, and to maintain that intimate touch with the personal life of his boys which gave his work its distinguishing mark. He knew each boy, his age and initials, the circumstances of his home life, the state of his work, and the nature of his interests. Over friendships he watched with especial vigilance. An incident quoted in Mrs. Ousey's biography will serve to illustrate all this. A boy had got completely across a master who perpetually ridiculed him, and the inevitable incident finally occurred. The master sent the boy to report to the Head.

' I did so,' writes the victim, ' with perfect confidence that I had a good case. The Head listened and then went right off (without reproving me over that) on to question of my friendships.

' To say that I was astonished at his intimate knowledge of these is to put it very mildly. As it happened my best friend had given me the go by and joined a sort of clique among whom I was not welcomed and so I had taken up with an irresponsible, hare-brained, but rather attractive boy as my pal. The Head knew all this and how jealousy and loneliness had been sapping my working energies ; and more, he knew that I was unconsciously in need of responsibility of some kind to give me an interest in school life again.

' He stood with his hand on my shoulder at the window of his study and talked in such a fatherly and homely manner about my people's wishes and hopes for me and the responsibilities of life that the tears rolled down my cheeks with no feelings of school-boy shame.

' He made me a " Scrip. Steward "[*] and I enjoyed it to the full, and many a time since have I blessed the day that I had to report to him. It sowed the seed of a permanent desire for voluntary work in addition to the day's normal task ; and has led to many honorary secretaryships and official positions connected with various organizations, charitable and otherwise. And I always look upon that wise appointment as the beginning of it all.'

—*McClure of Mill Hill*, pp. 90–91.

Is it a wonder that the boys loved their great Headmaster, that the roughest among us was constantly

---

[*] ' The Scrip ' at Mill Hill is the Reading Room, originally the Scriptorium of Dr. Murray after he left for Oxford, and now the building which commemorates his work.

subdued to affectionate reverence, and that we bear the mark of his love upon us for life ? The devotion of Old Millhillians to their School is proverbial. Of those who would have loved Mill Hill the more because of McClure, only too many fell in

> some corner of a foreign field
> That is forever England.

Others, who came out of the holocaust of the Great War, may well have felt a strange yearning to find again a love as spacious and as deep as his.

That love was often sorely tried, but it never failed. It is one thing to be a great organizer and a skilful teacher ; it is quite another thing to care deeply that every boy who comes to you should make good, and to go on believing that he can and will do so, even when the boy has lost faith in himself or never had any to lose. This was the daily and hourly sacrifice which McClure made for his boys, and with rare exceptions they knew it, and eventually responded. There are men throughout the world who know that they came through because ' The Bird ' believed in them.

The greatest trial of his faith and love came in the years of War. All schools were difficult to steer through those storm-tossed days ; and to one who had watched over his boys with more than a father's love, it was agony to see them cut off by the score in the bloom of their young manhood. Yet his faith never wavered. ' He was a man of simple and unwavering faith in God and humanity,' wrote his secretary.

' His was " a faith beyond the forms of faith," so that he was confident of final issues even in the darkest hour. I shall never forget the morning when news of the destruction of the *Lusitania* was in the papers. The first thing that struck me as I entered his study that morning was the grief in his face ; and then came the quick word of comfort as, looking at me sadly but very kindly, he said : "Aye, aye, we're up against it. It looks very dark, very dark—but always remember this, Miss Hill, ' The Lord reigneth,' aye, ' The Lord reigneth.' " '

McClure passed away in the fifth week of the Spring Term of 1922. He taught in school on the Saturday, preached at Highgate on the Sunday, and passed away on the next Saturday. The great host of Old Boys and friends who gathered to bid him a last farewell will always bear with them two memories : the sight of the Gate of Honour, its marble columns inscribed with the names of all Old Boys who fell for Britain, standing open, the broad terrace round it covered with wreaths ; and the last service in the Chapel which he had seen built, and which had become so identified in our minds with the thought of him. The funeral service was printed, not in black, but in the school colours, with his plain name

JOHN DAVID McCLURE

He was just a Millhillian, just one of us; and the great company which filled the pews and galleries, vestibule and aisles, and flowed out beyond the open doors on to

SIR JOHN McCLURE OF MILL HILL

the grass outside, joined with one voice in the great song of triumph

> Finita jam sunt proelia,
> Est parta jam victoria
> Gaudeamus et canamus
> Alleluia !

THE TEACHER'S REWARD

'TO the members of the hardest worked, the least advertised, the worst paid and the most richly rewarded profession.' Thus Major Ian Hay Beith, schoolmaster and novelist, dedicated his delightful book *The Lighter Side of School Life.* There are doubtless teachers throughout the world who would heartily endorse his definition of their profession, and in Britain at least, there has been a constant succession of able men and women willing to dedicate themselves to a life lived for young people. During this century a growing unity of ideals amongst teachers of varying types, and a willingness to act as members of an organized profession, have resulted in a relatively large rise in salaries; but even now the remuneration offered a teacher is very modest, and compels him to seek the reward of his work in higher realms, for which the only qualification is nobility of heart and mind. The teacher who has the true teacher's gift for sympathy with less enlightened natures, and who regards his pupils, and their parents, as friends to be cherished and served throughout life, will find that he has indeed entered into Kings' Treasuries and Queens' Gardens. Like John Wesley, he will have the world for his parish, and live in a realm whose boundaries are the five continents and the seven seas.

'There is no profession in which a man's virtues,

THE TEACHER'S REWARD

considered as moral levers, have so much purchase,' said McClure of Mill Hill, who had set aside the possibility of a brilliant career at the Bar to become a schoolmaster, and who declared at the end that, could he have his life again, he would again devote it to teaching. The teacher who can become what Dr. Morton of Leeds has aptly called a ' boy-man ' (or *mutatis mutandis*, a girl-woman) has an unparalleled opportunity to uplift the thought-models of mankind. Through the medium of teaching, and by the experiences of the school-journey, hike or trek, he or she can also sow broadcast the seeds of international friendship.

Dr. Morton has written in his *Hike and Trek*: ' The significance of our foreign friendship and good will cannot be over-estimated. . . Has boyhood no charm to save the future manhood of the race from the lion-spirit of hate that goes scurvily about seeking whom he may devour ? We believe it has . . . . Boyhood is generous. Boyhood has ideals. Boyhood has a sense of humour. Above all, boyhood has happiness. And the world catches these things and radiates them back to us, so that there is called forth that fellow-feeling and generous impulse which helps both sides to see the best in each other.'

The teacher has also the privilege, granted to but few today, of living among those whose interests are intellectual and artistic, and having, for some three months a year, the leisure which enables one to travel, read, paint, and write, or enjoy the quiet pleasures of the home.

SHAPERS OF MEN

His or her working days will be crowded and exacting ; it is a question if any task makes such demands on sheer personal energy as does schoolteaching, especially when this is combined with outdoor activities. To capture the heart of youth, one must live in tune with its boundless love of action, and there is little or no leisure for the teacher during the school term. The reward, however, is tremendous ; as Lord Baden Powell says, one constantly renews one's own youth in caring for the rising generation. It is no small privilege to live amid the hopefulness, spontaneity and overflowing good will of young people.

The highest reward will always come to the teacher who cares most wisely for the spiritual growth of his pupils. If in any country the teaching profession fails to progress, or to secure its rightful place in the community, one may feel sure that it has forgotten that, as a former Headmaster of Eton has written, ' if a boy is not daily coming to know God, the whole process is a failure.' Striving to emphasize this fact before an audience of London teachers, Stanley Baldwin once quoted those words from D'Arcy Thompson's *Day Dreams of a Schoolmaster* : ' Enlightened by the experience of fatherhood, they (the former pupils) will see with a clear remembrance firmness in dealing with their moral faults or patience in dealing with their intellectual weakness, and, calling to mind the old schoolroom, they will think it was good for us to be there. For unknown to us there therein were three tabernacles—one for us,

THE TEACHER'S REWARD

one for our schoolmaster, and one for Him Who is the friend of all children and the Master of all schoolmasters.' The teacher who is faithful in the Christian education of young people will have the greatest of all rewards, for he will find that he is indeed taught of God.

SPORT

COWES WEEK

BRITAIN abounds in beauty. There is a beauty of the Highlands and another of Snowdon; a beauty of the Broads and another of the Lakes; a beauty of Dartmoor and another of the New Forest; a beauty of great estuaries and another of land-locked harbours. Each county and each stretch of coast has its own beauty. But I remember none to compare with that of Cowes when King George and Queen Mary graced its Week with their presence.

I have been privileged to see Cowes Week from many standpoints. From the low deck of a pleasure-steamer, whose captain threaded his way between the racing yachts with a skill worthy of the finest yachtsman; from the towering decks of the *Milwaukee*, when Germans and Americans gazed at the glorious scene, and interpreted the mighty bulk of the attendant battleship for warning to keep off, instead of as a welcome to all to come in safety; from the verandah of one of those tiny hotels which nestle under the steep hillside, whence we saw the white hulls and sails of the yachts gleaming against the black sides of giant liners; most appealing of all, from the packed promenade by the landing stage of the Royal Yacht Squadron, where the crowd thickened by unerring instinct whenever Their Majesties were coming ashore.

SPORT

For the true magic of Cowes Week did not lie in the sparkling waters of the Solent, the beauty of billowing sails, nor the majestic presence of the battle cruiser, the liners and the Royal Yacht. All these were but a setting. The magic of Cowes Week lay in something far more rare and wonderful, something which no other roadstead has ever boasted ; for here the King and Commoners of Britain met in mutual happiness. For one brief week King George V could be at sea again, and share his sport with his people. The man we loved was there as one of us.

Greatly as we all enjoyed the yachting—for the crowds on the pleasure steamers and the promenade enjoyed it fully as much as the owner-yachtsmen—our eyes were always looking out for *Britannia*, watching to see His Majesty go to or from her in the cutter, or bring the Queen to shore from the *Victoria and Albert*; our feelings—and I fully believe their feelings—were those of people united in a common happiness.

There is said to be a special Providence which watches over midshipmen. There certainly is one which watches over eager youngsters of all persuasions. One year we had the good fortune to take our boys to Cowes in Regatta week. Returning from the seafront after hours of packed adventure, my wife spied a little passage full of ropes, and spars, and sails. She could get no further. A clerk who came out of a doorway gave us permission to enter, and we all walked into Fairyland.

BRITANNIA: THE LAST RACE

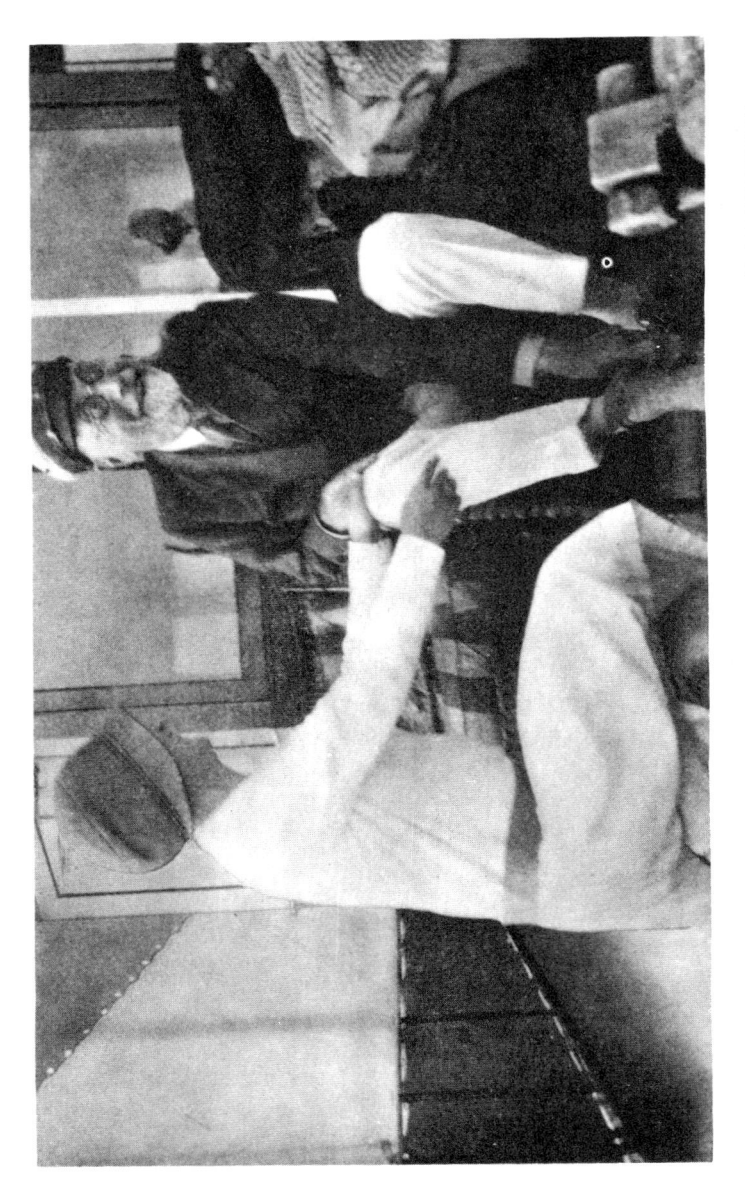

THOMAS RATSEY PRESENTING THE LUCKY SOCK TO MRS. FRANK ROBERTSON

At the end of the passage a door opened on to a balcony overhanging the harbour, with a launch fussing at her ropes below. On the balcony sat an elderly gentleman and two ladies. Somewhat abashed, we were retiring in good order; but we found ourselves cordially welcomed, and regaled with cakes and talk. After a while the gentleman of the party remarked that his launch was going out to his yacht. Perhaps we had time to go in her? Of course we had: so in we jumped and away we chugged down the Medina and out into the Solent. It was, I believe, in the launch that we discovered whom we had met. Our host was no other than the King's sailmaker, the late Mr. Thomas White Ratsey, a personal friend of His Majesty, who had superintended the making of all sails set by the *Britannia* since she was built in 1893. The yacht was the famous *Dolly Vardon*, on board of which King George and Queen Mary visited Mr. Ratsey during Cowes Week, 1934.

Mr. Ratsey, who passed away in 1935, was one of the best known yachtsmen of his long day, both in home waters and abroad, and was greatly beloved by the older members of the Royal Yacht Squadron. He enjoyed the distinction of being in all probability the only man whose right sock is preserved by a famous yacht club. This distinction came to him through having happily put his right sock on inside out, and worn it so throughout the final day's racing for the Seawanhaka Cup in Long Island Sound, on September 13th, 1929, when Mr. Frank Robertson's

8-metre *Caryl* won the Cup in the last ten seconds of the last race, after it had seemed certain that the American boat would win. Mr. Ratsey claimed the credit for the final puff of wind which proved decisive, and promptly took off his right sock and presented it to Mrs. Robertson. The sock is preserved by the Royal Northern Yacht Club.

When we returned to the balcony we took Mr. Ratsey into our confidence. We needed a sailing boat for our boys, and did not know where to go for one. He not only told us where a boat was being built, but asked his daughter to take us to the builder's yard. We bought the boat that night and ordered a Ratsey & Lapthorn sail as if we were America Cup-challengers.

Throughout our time on the island Mr. Ratsey continued to watch over our interests, warning us of dangerous water and advising safe stretches for the young sailsmen. Our boat is a small one, but it carries memories of a great English gentleman, and links us for life to Cowes, and to thoughts of Their Majesties.

CRICKETERS ALL

Joe's a player, and no mistake,
Comes to it born and bred,
Dines in pads for the practice' sake,
Goes with a bat to bed.
     EDWARD BOWEN.

IN a country which contains Neville Cardus, it seems impertinent to write about cricket or cricketers; yet no book on Britain would be complete which omitted the subject.

Cricket is the peculiar game of Britain; outside the Empire it is scarcely known, and to a foreigner it is inexplicable. 'Cricket,' said a Frenchman, 'is a game which the English have invented to express their idea of eternity.' Perhaps it is. When one passes from a noise- and gas-filled modern street into the quiet and spaciousness of a county cricket ground, one finds a peace and certainty that are hardly found elsewhere in everyday life.

Cricket is more than a game. It is the expression, in athletics, of chivalry and honour, and Johnny Tyldesley was perfectly right when he played cricket as if it were a religion. Nothing less can explain the extraordinary hold the game has on the imagination of the young, nor the profound meaning attached to the phrase, 'It wasn't cricket' or 'He doesn't quite play cricket.'

SPORT

Most English boys live for some hero of the cricket field, and my hero was Johnny Tyldesley; I am still looking forward to the day when my wife will take me to his childhood home, and show me the village green where J.T. learned the game. Not W. G. Grace, nor Archie MacLaren, nor C. B. Fry, nor even the great Ranji himself meant so much to me as Johnny, and many a weary day I kept myself up by thinking of him still in, and drawing even nearer to his next double-century. If there was one other batsman I cared about, it was the graceful R. H. Spooner, and of bowlers, Walter Brearley fascinated by his devil-may-care freedom on the field.

I shall never forget the first time I was taken to see a first-class match. The father of a school friend took us both to the Crystal Palace to see Australia *v.* The Gentlemen of England in April or May, 1904. I felt as if I were on Olympus; there at last were Victor Trumper, and Archie Maclaren, and the great Jessop himself. I walked on air.

When I passed from a private to a public school, fortune favoured me. I had good luck in the Freshers' Trial match, and was put in the Colts set under D. L. Morgan, who played twice for Gloucestershire within a week or so of leaving Mill Hill, then promptly left for India, where he took up polo. 'D.L.' was small and dark-skinned, and like a Greek god when stripped; he was the most perfectly proportioned lad and one of the best all-round athletes I have seen. He had his ' First Colours ' at all four games, and won the Average Bat for five years in succession, generally with an average of over 60. His drives and cuts were like a shot from a gun. At single-handed hockey, a Mill Hill game played with a stout ash stick, he would shatter four sticks in a forty-minute match : a stick lasted most players a month. His cricket strokes were of like power, but extremely graceful. He was a superb cover-point, and a useful bowler, but it was his batting that crowned all, and when we came out of school to watch the XI, we used to spy through the trees afar off to catch the first sight of his dark face at the wicket, and if it was there we knew all was well.

His greatest fighting innings only a dozen of us saw. We were playing St. Paul's School for the first time, on their own ground, and there was considerable speculation as to how we should fare against a school so much larger than our own, and with a great reputation behind it. At Mill Hill we lived on telegrams. Lunch-time, St. Paul's 60 for eight wickets ; we were in heaven. Then two of their men—one a nephew of G. K. Chesterton—made a century each, and by mid-afternoon they had made 271 all out. We lived for the telegraph boy. As the long afternoon dragged on the excitement grew greater and greater. Morgan was still in. The score was rising steadily, with the occasional loss of a wicket. Finally the result came through. Mill Hill 273 for nine, Morgan 170 not out.

The School house at Mill Hill is massively built, with spacious stone corridors ; it holds 130 boys, and the approach is up a drive commanded by dormitory windows. Only one sound in English history can quite have equalled the roar which greeted Morgan as the coach drew in, and that was the long-withheld first broadside at Trafalgar. The great building seemed to rock with the cheering. Morgan was seized, lifted shoulder-high and whirled along the pillared hall and down the corridor to his study as if on a torrent. Let down at last, he quietly took off his hat to us, smiled, and disappeared into his study. Not even that welcome could disturb his coolness, or give him the slightest vestige of self-consciousness. He was a true cricketer.

Oxford brought one into touch with plenty of fine cricketers, and the Army added some more. I was lucky to find myself in a mess with the Denton twins of Northamptonshire, whom I had not met before, though they were great friends of my eldest brother. The Dentons were slight and delicate-looking; they had, in fact, taken up County Cricket for their health, though it is not recorded what effect they had on the health of their opponents. It was often a case of

> Came the bowler and asked him, ' Pray,
> Shall I bowl you fast or slow ? '
> But the bowler's every hair was grey,
> Before he had done with Joe.

Once at Leytonstone the twins scored some 250 for the first wicket against Essex, and W.H. went on batting until lunch-time the next day. They were so alike that the scorers rarely knew which was which, and when they were asked to dress differently they used to exchange the 'get up' for fun, so that the records put down to them are often unlike the facts. Probably they are the only people who ever outwitted Wisden. Their younger brother Donald promised to be even more brilliant, but he lost a leg in the war, and though he played for the County at times with one leg, he has given it up. Business claims the twins now, but they are still the despair of local bowlers at the week ends.

Leaving the Army for school work, I expected to be a triton among the minnows, but already two of the boys who learnt cricket at our Wycliffe nets have played in a Gentlemen *v.* Players match, and one of them, Barnett of Gloucestershire, has played for England. Gloucestershire used to mean W. G. Grace; today it means Hammond. There is a good story told about one of the outlying parts of the county which is surrounded by Worcestershire territory. To simplify administration, it was proposed to transfer this district to Worcestershire, but the consent of the ratepayers had to be obtained. All consented but one old man, who was prepared for the change only if they could take Hammond with them!

The fascination of cricket lies in its uncertainty. In the year following the first Mill Hill *v.* St. Paul's match, our innings against University College School produced a like tension in reverse. University College School had the giant Susskind still with them, and

SPORT

their bowling proved unplayable ; six of our wickets were down for eight runs. Then Gerald Spicer, the son of Sir Evan Spicer, and Alan Knott, whose father was secretary of the Baptist Missionary Society, got together at the wicket. Very slowly they dug themselves in. Every ball was watched as if the fate of England depended on it. Ten was signalled, twenty, thirty, forty, fifty, sixty, seventy, eighty, ninety. Alan Knott's famous leg-scoop was in full play, and the partnership ended at 97. Susskind was now a mere name, and the tail wagged merrily, A. N. Scott of Rochdale, and the wicket-keeper, R. W. Atchley, putting on sixty or seventy for the last wicket. Unfortunately Susskind was missed from a very high catch, and the game fizzled out in a draw ; but the recovery was one only equalled by that against the M.C.C. in 1906, when after a disastrous start H. E. Snell, now a man of might in the Fiji Islands, and N. E. P. Harris, of Staffordshire, got together and made 39 each against the bowling of A. E. Relf, R. Relf, and Cox of Sussex, with Board behind the stumps.

The most remarkable finish I have seen—except perhaps the tie between Middlesex and Essex at Lords in 1910—was that on the Wycliffe ground between Wycliffe and Kingswood School, Bath, in 1927. We had an American Rhodes Scholar staying with us at home, and strolled down after tea to give him an idea of our national game. It was a wettish day with a sloppy ball. We found a tense silence on the ground which reminded one of Newbolt's :

CRICKETERS ALL

> There's a breathless hush in the Close to-night—
> Ten to make and the match to win—
> A bumping pitch and a blinding light,
> An hour to play and the last man in.

Kingswood had scored one hundred exactly, and Wycliffe were about 10 runs behind with two wickets in hand. The score crept to within three of the opponents' total, and the last over arrived. Jumping out boldly at the fifth ball, the batsman drove straight for the pavilion ; long-on, dashing round the railings, flung himself at the ball and stopped it *with his arm touching the railings*, then threw in and just prevented the batsman running three. The visiting umpire signalled a boundary, but the home umpire refused to give one ; off the last ball the batsman was neatly stumped ; and the match was left as a draw, Wycliffe being one run behind, with one wicket in hand.

The American carried away the feeling that there was a game even more exciting than baseball.

Cricket is part of the summer and part of England, or rather of the Empire. The most wonderful fact about it is that India has given us some of our finest players. When one watched the exquisite deftness of Ranji or Duleepsinjhi, one felt that India would eventually pull together with us, and bring its grace and agility to balance the sturdiness and strength of our national character. Cricket produces an atmosphere in which differences of race and rank vanish.

This unifying power of cricket has more than once helped me through a difficult task. While an undergraduate at Oxford I attended the Swanwick Camp of the Student Christian Movement and was deputed to act as camp host to the distinguished guests from the Hostel. Each evening one or more of these would come down to our Camp and share our supper of bread and cheese and mugs of cocoa. One night it fell to me to entertain Bishop Talbot of Winchester, the father of Neville Talbot, now Bishop of Pretoria, and of Gilbert Talbot, who was President of the Oxford Union Society. Gilbert fell only too soon after in No Man's Land, and Neville rescued his body under heavy fire, a deed commemorated in the name Toc H, or Talbot House. Anyone who remembers Bishop Talbot, a tall man of massive and imposing countenance, will be able to guess how shy I felt, especially as I was not an Anglican churchman. Fortunately there were little groups of men about the camp playing cricket ; and as the Bishop leant heavily on my arm—he was rather lame—he chatted to me of ' the great days in the distance enchanted ' when he and his brothers used to play with the famous Lyttleton brothers, several of whom entered first-class cricket. So, ' swopping lies about cricket,' the venerable Bishop and the shy young Baptist forgot the Act of Uniformity, and Cavalier and Roundhead shook hands in a cordial good-bye.

DOERS AND DREAMERS

C. T. STUDD, CRICKETER AND MISSIONARY

THE British are a practical people, intent on solid success, but there is always a spark of divine fire at work in the nation. Sir Arthur Quiller-Couch has recorded his observation that we only speak and write well when the Bible is constantly read among us; and we are incapable of living for long periods without a strong stirring of spiritual forces. The early 1870's were not distinguished for their spiritual fervour; they were the hey-day of hunting, the turf and country house cricket, and no household was more devoted to these sports than that of Edward Studd, whose three sons—Kynaston, George and Charles—were all in the Eton XI of 1877. Edward Studd was a retired Indian planter, a racer of fine horses and the owner of a private cricket ground at Tedworth (now Tidworth) in Wiltshire. His three sons had been almost born in the saddle, and were to make a great reputation as cricketers. One, Sir Kynaston, has recently been Lord Mayor of London and President of the M.C.C.

In the year 1875 a remarkable event occurred in the family. The father was converted at a Sankey and Moody meeting in Drury Lane Theatre. He sold his racers, barring three which he gave to the three boys as hunters, and threw himself into evangelistic work. The boys were dumbfounded. Their father was bent on their salvation and they were bent on escaping. Eventually a missioner whom he had invited down for the week-end cornered each of them separately and made them see the hollowness of their conventional Christianity. The effect on Kynaston was very deep; in George and Charles seeds were sown which came up later.

The fact is that Charles' religion was cricket. He used to practise keeping a straight bat for hours before the mirror in his bedroom. His enthusiasm was such as to provoke ridicule, but he stuck to his guns. Before he left Cambridge he was admittedly one of the two finest all-round cricketers—A. G. Steel being the other—in England. In the bowling averages he was second only to the professional Peate, and *Lillywhite's Annual* stated: ' Mr. C. T. Studd must be given the premier position amongst the batsmen of 1882, and it would be difficult to instance three finer innings played by so young a cricketer against the best bowling of the day than his three-figure scores against Australia and the Players.' He played for England *v.* Australia that summer, and also in the same winter overseas. England were beaten for the first time at the Oval, but won two of the three matches in Australia; with this defeat and victory began the legend of ' the Ashes.'

The next year was likewise one of triumph ; the *Cricketing Annual* accorded him for the second year in succession the premier position as an all-round player. He also won the Cambridge single Racquets match and represented the Varsity against Oxford. By 1884 each of the three brothers had captained the University XI in succession, and *Punch* nicknamed them the ' set of Studds.'

At the height of his fame Charles Studd found himself watching by the side of what threatened to be his brother George's death-bed. In these solemn hours the transitory nature of all earthly fame came forcibly to him. He went to see Moody, and during the next season persuaded several of the England XI to hear the evangelist, who made a lasting impression on the captain, the Hon. Ivo Bligh (later Lord Darnley) and on A. G. Steel ; A. J. Webbe, Oxford and England, remained one of Studd's closest friends throughout life, and among those who were profoundly influenced by his brother Kynaston was Sir William Grenfell of Labrador.

As his spiritual life deepened and became more definite and powerful, Charles Studd felt led to go to China as a missionary. He met with strong opposition from his own family, and many of his religious friends said that he was throwing away his life-work. Such a man, they felt, would be a great force for good among students in Britain. Once more Studd stuck to his guns ; with Stanley Smith, stroke of the Cambridge Eight, and five other Cambridge men he prepared to go to China ; and as it turned out, the meetings they held at the Universities and elsewhere before their departure lit the torch of a great spiritual movement among the students.

DOERS AND DREAMERS

'The Cambridge Seven' went out to live as Chinamen among the Chinese. After two years Studd took a step which was decisive for his whole career. Pondering deeply on the incident of Christ Jesus and the rich young ruler, he decided to give away his whole fortune and trust entirely in God for his supplies. The decision was not made hurriedly. On January 13th, 1887, he sent off four cheques of £5,000 and four of £1,000 for various religious and charitable purposes. Shortly afterwards he gave several more thousands. In his humorous way he remarked that an hundredfold had been promised in this life to those who left all for Christ, and that an hundredfold was 10,000 per cent, a very good rate of interest.

To take such a step was inherent in Charles Studd's whole character. His spiritual life had become all to him, and he found this spiritual life enriched in proportion as he set aside all other considerations to spread the gospel message among those who had had no possible chance to hear it. His life in China already offered him far more than life in England had done—greater opportunities, more adventure, and above all a closer walk with God. After he had given away his fortune it became richer still, and the enrichment was a direct result of the giving.

One of the larger cheques had been sent to the Salvation Army to aid its work in India. It arrived when it was most needed, and made possible a considerable reinforcement of new workers from home. As a result, Booth Tucker wrote to Studd a glowing letter about their work in India, describing the opportunities which opened as they gave up European habits and lived as natives. Hearing that his brother George was to be in Shanghai, Charles Studd came over from the West of China, bringing the letter with him. One day after prayers he asked if he might read this letter to the little group of workers at the Sailors' Home. Among the workers was a beautiful young Irish girl from Lisburn near Belfast, a Miss Priscilla Stewart. Eighteen months earlier she had given up the society life which was all to her, and had eventually come out as a missionary; but the shock of the change had been too great, and she had developed heart trouble. Booth Tucker's letter changed her whole outlook; she literally took new heart, physically and mentally, and from a listless semi-invalid became the life and soul of the work at the Sailors' Home. George Studd wrote home to his mother: ' There is a Miss Stewart here who has lately come out to the mission and has been wonderfully used of God. Doors have been opened to her right and left, and in several houses she has been the means of bringing people on to their knees in drawing rooms where I do not suppose anyone ever knelt to the Lord before.' George himself had come out to Shanghai to play cricket and so forth ; he remained for a time in China as a fellow-worker with his brother, and finally gave his life to evangelical work in California, where he is today. And before six months had passed Priscilla Stewart had become Mrs. Charles Studd. The price of a virtuous woman is above rubies, and the young missionary had received his 10,000 per cent.

Upon his marriage he deeded to her the last remnant of his fortune, and she promptly sent it to General Booth, with the request that the gift be kept anonymous. Then with five dollars and a roll of bedding, the young couple started out, in company with a Miss Burroughes, to open work in the inland city of Lungang-Fu, where there were no Europeans.

The only house they could get was a haunted one. Every calamity which occurred in the city was blamed on 'the foreign devils,' and for five years they were greeted everywhere with a volley of curses. On one occasion they were only just saved from death at the hands of a mob. But they persevered and won through. The Opium Refuge which Mr. Studd organized became the means of saving hundreds of ruined men and women, and after the first three months they experienced remarkable results in their evangelical work. Five children were born to them, without doctor or nurse, and four grew into healthy children ; one they lost as a babe. After the birth of the first child an incident occurred which is of great historic value. Mrs. Studd became dangerously ill, and was nursed by a lady missionary of some medical experience who arrived after some days. One night all seemed lost. Miss Kerr, the helper, said that if the patient did survive she must leave China. This roused Mr. Studd ; nothing must interfere with their work for China ; and he proposed to follow the instructions given in James v, verses 14 and 15. Miss Kerr would not accept the responsibility, but Mrs. Studd welcomed the idea ; so Mr. Studd anointed her with oil and prayed. Immediately the trouble ceased, and when Miss Kerr came the next morning she found her patient healed.

At another time the young couple found themselves wholly without funds. Starvation stared them in the face. They decided to spend the night in prayer, but after twenty minutes felt relieved, and went to bed. A fortnight later the mail arrived, but the letters from the bag contained nothing. Mr. Studd turned the bag upside down and shook it. Out came a letter in an unknown hand, and in it a cheque for £100, sent by a man they did not know, who stated that for reasons unknown to him he felt commanded to send them this money. It is worth noting that in the course of their work Mr. and Mrs. Studd received for their work in such ways about five times the amount of the fortune which they had surrendered.

The one critical moment in the seven years at Lungang-Fu came after the loss of the babe. The couple were absolutely alone, and when the husband went out to buy a box for a coffin the young mother was broken-hearted. She faced the question whether she was to give in and let her life as a missionary be ruined. Then she made a covenant with God that no sorrow of any kind should spoil her work, and when her husband returned he never saw a tear. It is little wonder that, when they finally left the city in

1894, they were accompanied to the first village by a great procession of grateful Chinese.

In England they were lovingly received by Charles' mother. Both were broken in health, but the husband returned to activity as soon as possible. His brother Kynaston had conducted a most successful evangelistic campaign in the American Universities, which had given rise to the Student Volunteer Movement and brought John R. Mott into the work ; Charles now followed by a tour which brought new life to many. Later he went to India, where, after working among the planters who had known his father, he accepted the pastorate of the Union Church, Ootacamund, Southern India, a charming hill-station to which the government officials of Madras migrated in the hot weather. His wife and family followed him, and the Studds spent busy but happy years in Ootacamund. The place was ideal for the girls, and the parents enjoyed society suited to them. They were often invited to Government House by Lord and Lady Ampthill, Lord Ampthill being an Old Etonian ; while staying with them in Madras Charles T. Studd met Lord Kitchener; and at Ootacamund he had a long chat with Lord Curzon. He took up cricket again, and made two double-centuries in one season, a feat only once before performed in India. He was very successful as a pastor among the most varied types of Europeans and Eurasians. In 1906, however, asthma of increasing severity compelled a return to England.

Here he was quickly at work again, speaking for all

manner of organizations to tens of thousand of men who probably never went to church, but who were drawn by the appeal of an address from a famous cricketer. To the great joy of the parents, supporters paid for all four daughters to be educated at Sherborne and later, in the case of three, at Lausanne, and their grandmother took them for the holidays. A still greater joy was the enthusiasm of the girls for the work of evangelisation.

In 1908 Charles Studd was in Liverpool. He was still contemplating a return to India, when he saw a placard inscribed ' Cannibals want Missionaries.' The unconscious humour of the statement appealed to him, and he went inside to find who had put up the notice. As he expected, he found a foreigner, a Dr. Karl Kumm, who had walked across Africa. From him Studd learnt of the great populations to whom no one had ever gone with the message of Christ Jesus' life. He determined to go, but the difficulties seemed insuperable. The business men who first promised support withdrew it when the doctor forbade the journey. And, worst of all, his wife did not approve. Nevertheless he booked a passage to Port Said. On the first night on board the Bibby liner he went to his cabin and there received this startling message from God : ' This trip is not merely for the Sudan, it is for the whole Unevangelised World.' It is a fact that the Worldwide Evangelisation Crusade began with that voyage to Africa.

Charles Studd was filled with new life and vigour.

He was convinced that his wife's health would be restored, and that she and his daughters would join him. ' The doctors would have frightened me into my grave long ago, had I paid attention to them, but I live, and live by faith in Jesus and the power of God. You must do the same,' he wrote to her from Marseilles. The story of the Heart of Africa Mission, which broadened into the Worldwide Evangelisation Crusade with its missions in the most difficult spots in the world, is told in Mr. Norman P. Grubb's *C. T. Studd.* It is a dramatic story, worthy of the New Testament, a story of penetration into unknown lands, of dangers, victories, set-backs and recoveries. Mr. Studd returned to England after a preliminary survey, and his wife came over to his side before he finally set out on a planned campaign in 1913. Once again she had a terrible battle with sorrow, and once again she won the day. But she grew increasingly ill after he sailed, and her heart was found to be extended by several inches. The doctor sentenced her to live quietly for the rest of her life ; but she was soon organizing support from her bed, and when her husband returned after two years he found a well-equipped Headquarters had been established by his wife and daughters at 17 Highland Road, Upper Norwood, still the centre for the work. In two years one physical wreck had blazed a trail of missionary work through the heart of Africa, and another had organized the home front.

During his trek to the Heart of Africa with Alfred

Buxton, a Cambridge man who had started with him when under twenty-one, Studd had many remarkable experiences. One of these he related in my own home, where I met him during his last furlough. Stricken with fever, and apparently dying, he had been healed overnight when Buxton anointed him with oil and prayed; the oil had been taken from their kerosene lamp! It had been expected that the Belgians would prevent the work, but Count Ferdinand de Grunne, a Roman Catholic government official, proved to be a magnificent friend and ally. Later, Studd was made a Chevalier of the Royal Order of the Lion by the King of the Belgians. On one occasion he found that he had passed the night unhurt with a peculiarly deadly snake in his blankets. Among a people cannibal, totally ignorant, steeped in vice and sorcery, he had been welcomed and protected and listened to. His power lay in his complete renunciation of self, in his absolute obedience to and trust in the guidance of the Holy Spirit. ' The difficulty is to believe that He can deign to use such scallywags as us, but of course He wants faith and fools rather than talents and culture. All God wants is a heart, any old turnip will do for a head; so long as we are empty all is well, for then he fills us with the Holy Ghost ', he wrote in the Movement's magazine.

Charles Studd went back to Africa and worked to the end, two of his daughters coming to work with him. The hardest thing he had to bear was the separation from his wife, who had overcome her invalidism and become the main organiser of the campaign. Only once, for a fortnight in 1928 did she manage to visit him. That visit taught the native Christians a lesson. They saw with their own eyes what it had cost to win them. Three years later Charles Studd lay in his bamboo hut dying. To the end he was concerned about his fellow workers and his converts. At those moments in which he could spare breath he kept uttering one word, ' Hallelujah.' It was his last written and his last spoken word—' Hallelujah.'

CHARLES STUDD IN AFRICA

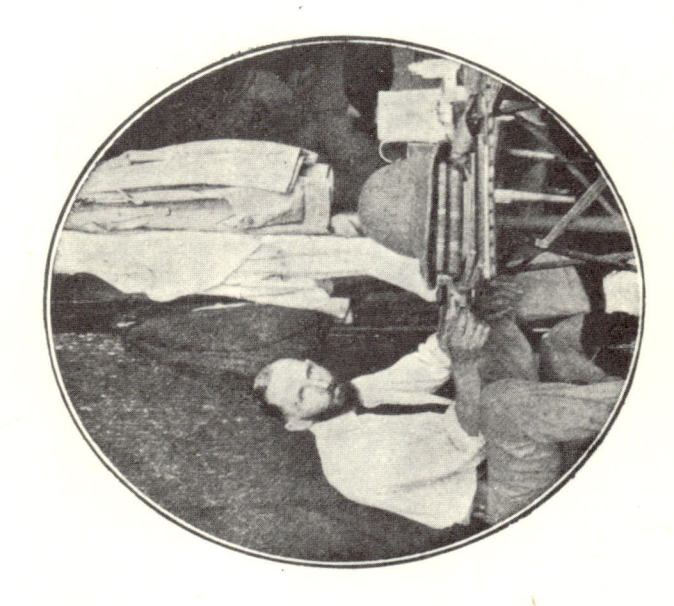

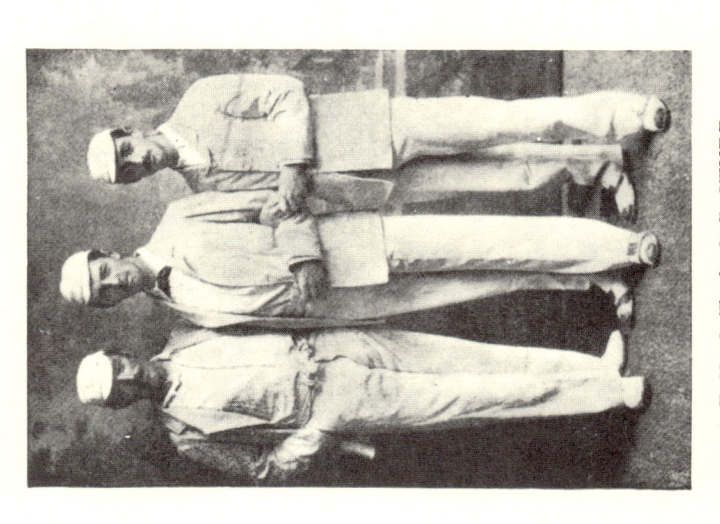

J. E. K., C. T. & G. B. STUDD
Eton XI 1877, Cambridge XI 1881-2,
Captains of Cambridge successively, 1882-3-4
C. T. & G. B. : All England XI 1882-3

SYDNEY DOBELL

SYDNEY DOBELL

THE name of Sydney Dobell is so little known today that the passage from *Balder* quoted at the close of this book may come as a complete surprise to the reader, who cannot but be struck by the passionate love of England and by the mastery of her language which it displays.

Sydney Dobell was born in Kent in 1824, of an old Sussex cavalier family; his mother was the daughter of Samuel Thompson, an ardent political, social and religious reformer, founder of a Church which endeavoured to return to primitive Christianity. Its members eschewed all social intercourse with those outside their own communion. John Dobell, the father, became an adherent of 'the Church,' and the son was brought up at home according to its strictest precepts. Owing to his parents' strong views he never went to school or college, and at the age of twelve entered the family wine business, which was then established at Cheltenham.

Such were the conditions in which the young poet began life; yet his natural ability, his innate nobility of character, and his considerable social gifts soon won him the friendship of the most cultured residents in a town long known as an intellectual centre. Sir Arthur Broom Faulkner, traveller and man of letters, was the most intimate of his friends, and the poet Campbell was attracted to him. To wide and varied reading he added a constant study of nature in all her moods ; and the religious earnestness of his family reached its highest development in the young poet, who, compelled to spend much of his day in the counting-house, gave his nights to prayer and to profound meditation on the Scriptures. His parents were alarmed at his habits, and begged him to relax his religious exercises ; but despite the strain on his health, the young man refused. In one of his poems he has told us what prayer meant for him :

> On a solemn day
> I clomb the shining bulwark of the skies :
> Not by the beaten way,
> But climbing by a prayer,
> That like a golden thread hung by the giddy stair
> Fleck'd on the immemorial blue.
> By the strong step-stroke of the brave and few,
> Who, stirr'd by echoes of far harmonies,
> Must either lay them down and die of love,
> Or dare
> Those empyrean walls that mock their starward eyes.

This strong spiritual upthrust in his nature, coupled with the comparative seclusion of his early years, developed in him an intensity of devotion which made his parents hope that he would become the leading influence in ' The Church ' ; but as Dobell grew to manhood, the cavalier in his nature asserted itself. On the threshold of his career he was indeed a strange mixture of contradictions, refusing from principle to enter the houses of his cultured friends, but entertaining them with the warmest hospitality in his own ; and uniting a passion for abstract thought with a growing interest in public affairs which soon transcended even his innate patriotism, and awoke in him the warmest sympathy with the Italian struggle for liberty.

His father wisely made over to him the independent management of a business branch in Gloucester. He was now married, and the young couple went to live at Lark Hay, in the village of Hucclecote. Here, during the summer of 1848, Sydney Dobell began a dramatic poem, *The Roman*. He had already decided to devote his main effort to poetry, which he regarded as a sacred bond between a man and his Maker.

The Roman was published in his twenty-fourth year under the pseudonym of Sydney Yendys, and won immediate recognition at home, in America and in Europe. The author, who had never left England, had caught the atmosphere of Italy as Schiller caught that of Switzerland in *William Tell*, and the passage on the Coliseum challenges comparison with that by Byron. No poem had been so widely read abroad since *Childe Harold*. The most exacting critics in Britain hailed the appearance of a new poet of the highest order ; and the author's generous enthusiasm for the Italian cause won for *The Roman* a wide public. The unknown young wine-merchant suddenly found himself the centre of international interest. He was awed and humbled, for he knew the limitations of his work, and saw that he must strive to fulfil its promise.

After a holiday in Switzerland he remained for a considerable time in London, where he was warmly welcomed by the leading writers of the day, among them Robert Browning, Coventry Patmore and George Macdonald ; later he won the friendship of Tennyson and Carlyle. Dobell's favourite brother Clarence was an artist, and his own powers of appreciation brought him into contact with Ruskin, Holman Hunt and Dante Gabriel Rossetti. With Charlotte Brontë he maintained a correspondence of marked literary value ; later, he made friends with the leading men of letters in Scotland, and so drank in the spirit of that country, that some of his finest short poems were written in the Scots dialect, and breathe the very spirit of the Highland clans.

Returning to Gloucestershire from London, he completed the first part of a trilogy on the artistic life. *Balder*, published in 1853, was a study in artistic egotism. It was not successful with the public, and was justly criticised for the painful nature of the plot; but its author rightly said ' There is as much poetry in many a chapter of *Balder* as in the whole of *The Roman*.' It will always remain a mine for poets, and one of the foremost writers of the day exclaimed : ' I have always thought that for deep-derived, far-reaching phraseology, and for the power of wielding such with perfect mastery in an atmosphere of passion, the highest mood of Dobell is closely akin to Shakespeare and Shelley.'

Two years later, in 1855, Dobell published with Alexander Smith a series of stirring sonnets on the Crimean War. Among them were two addressed to America which are of permanent interest, and were far in advance of the general thought of his day:

AMERICA.

Men say, Columbia, we shall hear thy guns.
But in what tongue shall be thy battle-cry?
Not that our sires did love in years gone by,
When all the Pilgrim Fathers were little sons
In merrie homes of Englaunde? Back, and see
Thy satchelled ancestor! Behold, he runs
To mine, and, clasped, they tread the equal lea
To the same village school, where side by side
They spell ' Our Father.' Hard by, the twin pride
Of that grey hall whose ancient oriel gleams
Thro' yon baronial pines, with looks of light
Our sister-mothers sit beneath one tree.
Meanwhile our Shakespeare wanders past and dreams
His Helena and Hermia. Shall we fight?

Nor force nor fraud shall sunder us? Oh ye
Who north or south, on east or western land,
Native to noble sounds, say truth for truth,
Freedom for freedom, love for love, and God
For God; oh ye who in eternal youth
Speak with a living and creative flood
This universal English, and do stand
Its breathing book; live worthy of that grand
Heroic utterance—parted, yet a whole,

> Far, yet unsevered,—children brave and free
> Of the great Mother-tongue, and ye shall be
> Lords of an Empire wide as Shakespeare's soul
> Sublime as Milton's immemorial theme,
> And rich as Chaucer's speech, and fair as Spenser's dream.

Later Dobell published a book entirely of his own entitled *England in Time of War*. It is full of delicate insight into the feelings of common people in England and Scotland, and was well received. These two books were his last, for failing health cut short his career. He had to relinquish all hope of producing another major work, and the poetic promise of his youth remained unfulfilled.

Where most men would have been broken by such a disappointment, Dobell rose superior to it. He returned to Gloucestershire, and developed an extensive branch of the family business designed to make of the firm a Commonwealth on co-operative lines, devoted to the well-being of all concerned. He took a lively interest in the literary, artistic and charitable organizations of Gloucester. His winters he spent in France and Italy, where he was welcomed with open arms. In summer he threw himself into the joys of English country life, and became known as a lover of horses and as the keeper of a rare and beautiful breed of deer-hounds. The cottagers round his home all knew him and experienced his generous interest. Whenever health permitted, he contributed to reviews and periodicals, and gave unstintingly of his counsel and of his slender wealth to struggling aspirants for literary honours. As strength declined, he seemed to grow gayer and more lighthearted, and to the last gathered round him a circle of devoted friends. His deep religious convictions were unimpaired by disappointed hopes or physical suffering. He belonged to no recognized denomination ; but among his memoranda were found these words, which express the essence of a religion beyond the grasp of creeds : ' Whatever things are true for Man the Immortal I call religion, and, in this sense, religion is the only worthy object of Human Study.'

' His real fascination,' wrote John Nicholl, ' lay in the incommunicable beauty of a character in which masculine and feminine elements, strength and tenderness, were almost uniquely blended. Manliness in its highest attributes of courage, energy and independence pervaded his life. It often occurred to us that Mr. Dobell would have made a great General ; he was absolutely without fear, and being under all circumstances perfect master of himself was pre-eminently fit to master and command others. He was, in fact, a true Englishman. The moral earnestness and religious intensity of the Puritan were blended in his nature with the joy of life and the generous human enthusiasm of the Cavalier ; to a passionate patriotism, and a love of all the sights and sounds of the English countryside, he united a glowing interest in the cause of freedom abroad, and a strong sense of brotherhood with the people of America.

In this, as in his social and economic views, he was far ahead of his day ; but his verse reflects also a warm sympathy with the contemporary feeling of his fellow-countrymen.

Lacking the advantage of classical culture, with all it means in precision and balance of language, he had read widely in English poetry, and the music of the English Bible was ever in his ears. As a lad, he had learned the New Testament by heart ; and its mingled strength and tenderness are the background of his thought.

Sydney Dobell was a poet in all that he did. His conception of the poet's mission was akin to that of Schiller, and in his thought poetry was never divorced from life. He wrote his first major work while in business as a wine merchant, and when further creative work was forbidden him, he cheerfully turned to the task of expressing his idealism in business. In his very last poem he summed up the message of his life work thus :

> To fulfil the Law
> In Gospel, force the seeds of use to flower
> In beauty, to enman invisible truth
> And thus transfigure—this is Poetry.

JOHN BELLOWS, FRIEND

SHOULD you ever chance to stray into the City Library of Gloucester, England, you may find among the biographies a stoutly rebound volume with much-thumbed pages, entitled *John Bellows, Letters and Memoir*. John Bellows was a Cornish Quaker who settled in Gloucester as a printer. He was a master of the Cornish dialect, and embarked upon a Dictionary of the dialect, which he abandoned on the appearance of *William's Dictionary*. His greatest work, both as a compiler and a printer, was his pocket *French Dictionary*. It was the first pocket dictionary for travellers, and won a well-deserved reputation throughout the English-speaking world. His pen and press also rendered notable service to the country in times of political crisis, and earned him the warm thanks of Lord Salisbury.

Amid the turmoil and distractions of a business career, John Bellows found time to spin threads of affection which bound in comradeship not only masters and men in his printing works, but an ever-widening circle of friends in many lands, extending at last from Russia to New England, and including within its bounds characters as diverse as Count Leo Tolstoy, the German archaeologist Dr. Hübner, and Prince Lucien Bonaparte, in Europe ; Lord Ducie, Leslie Stephen, and Professor Max Müller in England ;

Professor J. Stuart Blackie, in Scotland ; Oliver Wendell Holmes, Chief Justice Holmes, and Senator Hoar in America. The range of his friendships was due to the versatility of his mind, but the root and substance of all his dealings with others was John Bellows' ceaseless desire to be found the Friend of God. Amid the wonderful wealth of thought and feeling poured out in these Letters, the purest gold is ever to be found when he is speaking of man's relations with his heavenly Father. Whether he is wrestling with another's doubts, or encouraging a young soldier on his way to the front, or counselling one of his own children, or comforting an old friend in his loneliness, John Bellows has that sureness and gentleness of touch which can only flow from a deep and continuous inner experience of the Divine presence.

If there was one friend to whom, more than another, John Bellows opened the full range of his thought and feeling, it was to Oliver Wendell Holmes. It is wonderful to watch, as one after another of that great New England writer's friends passed from the scene, and Holmes was left alone to wrestle with the difficulties of the years, how his pathway was cheered by the rich outpouring of affection—and shall we not say genius ?— which inspired this remarkable series of letters, letters written under every imaginable difficulty, sometimes begun in one country and finished, months later, in another.

There are literary letters, inspired by the receipt of Holmes' latest volumes, gems of criticism set in delight-

ful descriptions of domestic happiness; archaeology has its place, for John Bellows was the discoverer of the Roman Wall of Gloucester and his archaeological and philological interests brought him wide repute and an honorary degree from Harvard University; travel is there in rich variety, for it was by a logical development that he invented the traveller's dictionary. His many visits to friends abroad, and the frequent response he made to an inner call to go on long missions of mercy into distressed countries, had brought him a great store of impressions upon which his intellect played with delightful humour and vivacity. His description of Russia and the Caucasus remain long in the memory, as do the scattered fragments of his conversation which light up the dark scene. As a parting remark to a Russian Princess he observed: ' I find *nearly everyone* in Russia believes that the Emperor is the highest power in the Empire—and after him comes the Governor of a Province—after the Governor comes the Ispravnik (Chief of Police) and *somewhere*, below the Ispravnik, comes the Almighty.' *
She came back into the room, seized his hand with a strong grip, and said ' You are *right.*'

Holmes had sent him *Over the Teacups*; and the book sets him pondering over the mystery of the boundary between manhood and boyhood . . .

' Only this very evening I was wheedled into an interlude from the *Teacups* by a deputation of four Gallios who

---

*This and subsequent quotations from letters are taken by permission from *John Bellows, Letters and Memoir, by his Wife.*

cared for none of these things, to entreat that I would " give them a chase." Seven-year-old put the request in a very low voice ; for a " chase " in this house is forbidden by the mistress on the ground that it makes a dust : it destroys the carpets : it leaves finger-marks on the walls : it tears the clothes : it upsets the furniture : with other high crimes and misdemeanours which are duly set forth in the manifesto which forbids chasing " indoors," and so
" a spirit in my feet
Has led me, who knows how "
out of the room, these four stealing after me, till we get to the foot of the front stairs, when off they go like hares, I following—into the bathroom, and the day-nursery, and the night nursery, and down the back stairs, for dear life ! Every one I catch is swept off to prison, either tucked under my arm, or dragged by the heels along the floor—according to size and weight. (It doesn't hurt the carpets a bit ! It's only a superstition of the mistress. They look fresher than ever after it !) . . . Boy ! Why, I was never more a boy in my life ! What boy in the whole world ever cared about carpets in the midst of a chase ? '

This man was clearly made to live at home, like Cowper, and cheer an English fireside. But the very next letter is likely to come from France, or the Russian Steppes, or Constantinople, or Tiflis, where he has gone to administer relief or defend the privileges of some persecuted sect. On these journeys he was sometimes accompanied by his wife, who was a wise counsellor and devoted companion throughout their married life. Even if he only goes to London, he is sure to have made friends with a young officer in the corner seat or by the boy who carried his bag, and to have pledged himself to some act of kindness which will mean putting aside his domestic pleasure. And he had his reward. Who of us would not have given much to have Tolstoy grasp both his hands and say with emotion : ' I have *great* love for you '; and to have found among his baggage a parcel of toys from Tolstoy's children to his children ?

The world is still awaiting an adequate biography of John Bellows. He was a man gifted with exceptional power to inspire his fellows. Lord Ducie, the Lord-Lieutenant of that time, who had known him for forty years and used to correspond with him in Norwegian, declared that he was so many-sided that no one man could be said to know him thoroughly. He was at his greatest in conversation, and Senator Hoar, friend of Whittier and Emerson and Oliver Wendell Holmes, felt him to be one of the half-dozen men whose spoken words should have been recorded ; he spoke also of the deep impression John Bellows made on those he met in America, many of whom looked back on their meeting with him as a memorable event. This remarkable gift for inspiring conversation he shared with Sydney Dobell. He shared also with the Dobells their profound interest in religion, and one of his finest letters is written to Mrs. Dobell on the subject of Prayer. It runs :

> ' The point thou has mentioned is the *vital* one : for Prayer is the very beginning and end of our true spiritual life : but not always prayer in words, or even in words

shaped in thought, but unuttered. If we are bidden to "pray without ceasing," it is evident that this must cover wider ground than speech or active thought.

'There is an attitude of mind as in the presence of God which I believe corresponds to this prayer without ceasing, and which is described in the Psalms, etc., as "Waiting upon the Lord." I recollect that my father, who was fond of the study of Hebrew, pointed out to me that the word in the original in such passages was "To be *silent unto* the Lord." "They that are *silent unto* the *Lord* shall *renew their strength*," etc.

'I had mentioned this to Count Tolstoi, in reference to something that occurred in our conversation. He was much interested in it; and fetching Young's Concordance he asked me to give him a passage in point. We turned to the closing portion of the 40th Isaiah, and as the chapter-division there happens to come in the wrong place, cutting off a verse that really belongs to, and completes the passage itself, we read on to the end of the first verse in Chapter 41.

'Count T. turned to the Hebrew, and said quietly, "Yes; it *is* so: *They that are silent unto the Lord* shall *renew their strength* : they shall mount up with wings as eagles," etc. "*Keep silence before Me*, O Islands, and *let* the people *renew their strength*."

'This is a deep matter; and I feel the danger of getting *beyond* my depth in touching on it; yet not to realize it is to lose the greatest help we can have in our spiritual course. To sink into the reverent silence of the will and of *self*, before the Almighty, is to " dwell in the secret place of the Most High," and to " abide under His shadow : " that is, to be in the closest communion with God that is possible for a human soul. This is the essence and foundation of prayer, whether words are given to us in utterance of it, or whether they are withheld; for there are times when the very withholding is but the means of enabling us more immediately to perceive the Divine voice—perhaps a still, *small* voice.

'I cannot add much ; but I am certain that no one who has once found the help and strength that are experienced in this, will ever again rest in any *lower* experience. It is a laying hold of the Power of the Almighty in times of trial, of storm, of temptation that threaten to destroy us ; and it was this, surely, that Solomon meant when he said, " *The Name* of the Lord is a strong tower : the righteous runneth into it, *and is safe.*" '

John Bellows was one of the last men to wear the Quaker garb and to use the Quaker plain speech; his firm still opens its business letters with the address ' Dear friend.' Broad as he was in his sympathies, no consideration would induce him to abandon the rules of the Society of Friends. His researches had convinced him that the north-western angle of the Roman Wall of Gloucester passed under the Cathedral, and he concluded that materials from it might be incorporated in the columns of the nave. As a Quaker, he believed it wrong to remove his hat when entering a church, and in consequence he never entered the Cathedral to verify his conclusions. He would face serious financial loss rather than give any but his best work to the world, and having decided to produce an improved second edition of his *French Dictionary*, he steadfastly refused to reprint the first, and for nearly four years denied himself the ample profits which he could readily have made by re-issuing the less perfect edition. A business based on such qualities thrives by its innate value. John Bellows gathered around him a fine body of craftsmen, and established such a reputation for the high quality of his printing that he could dispense almost entirely with modern methods and salesmanship. He was one of the delegates appointed by the Society of Friends to convey the Loyal Address to His Majesty King Edward VII on the occasion of the latter's accession to the Throne. In a letter to his son Philip, then in Philadelphia, John Bellows gives a delightful description of the scene at St. James's Palace:

Cheyne Walk, Chelsea, 12/3/1901.

'. . . . A buzz of conversation behind us gets a little too loud for etiquette, and an officer in front gives a gentle "*sh.*" This is not for the Friends, however: but for *Lord Roberts* and a little knot of officers just behind us, who are waiting their turn for some other deputation. Then the door opens, and we all move forward between the lines of life guards, to the front of the throne. The King, seated on it, is dressed in scarlet ; the Duke of Cornwall and York,* on his left, standing, is dressed in black with many stars and insignia on ; and a gentleman I cannot identify stands on the right of the throne. On either hand of these stand officers and life guards. Caleb Kemp steps slightly in advance, and reads—" May it please the King," and so on. The King stoops forward —and is evidently listening earnestly. He is touched— as I felt certain he would be. Caleb Kemp, in closing, explains that there are also some friends from Ireland among us, who, though they had no share in the address,

---

*Prince George, later H.M. King George V.

wish to identify themselves with its assurance of loyalty to himself and the throne, and with our desires for his welfare and that of his people. He rolls up the address and hands it to the King, who takes it and bows, and then passes it to an officer. The gentleman on his right then steps forward and places before him his written reply (for the King has previously read the address and prepared his answer), which he reads clearly and in a deep voice. It is beautiful—and expresses a hope that the principles Friends have striven for may spread during his reign, while he asks our prayers for his faithful fulfilment of the duties that fall to his lot as Sovereign. . . .

' I have given thee the outside state of things. To me it simply brought home the lesson, " The fashion of this world passeth away," and the feeling of how great and earnest the duty is of our sinking into exercise of soul that the King may be kept faithful to that renewed visitation of the Divine love which has, I am certain, been granted him in this time of sorrow at his mother's death, and in realization of the responsibilities that rests on him. As we do this we help him *to build for eternity.*'

In the same year in which this letter was written a noble portrait of him was painted by Percy Bigland. John Bellows passed away in May, 1902, and on January 6th of the next year an artist's copy of this portrait was formally presented to the City of Gloucester by his old friend Lord Ducie, on behalf of the subscribers. In reply the Mayor of the City, Dr. E. Sydney Hartland, made a memorable speech, which is preserved in the Centenary Tribute compiled by his son, John Earnshaw Bellows, and published in 1931.

A few lines from the speech make a fitting close to this chapter:

'... There was no mistaking him : he was John Bellows, and nobody else. His lean, tall figure, slightly bent, his quaint garb, his bright and earnest eyes, arrested the attention at once. When you got into conversation with him, no matter about what, his quiet manner, his old-world speech and courtesy, his wide knowledge and accurate memory, his readiness to listen, as well as to talk, his kindly witticisms, and his endless store of facts and anecdotes, constituted an unbounded charm. Further acquaintance made known a character of the deepest and most solemn convictions, sharply defined beliefs carried out in daily life with punctual and even ritualistic formality, but all controlled and brought into harmony by an overflowing kindliness, a spontaneous love for his fellow-men that impelled him not merely to avoid offence, but to seek for their highest good. It was a revelation. You felt that a new planet, as brilliant as unexpected, had swum into your ken. You had found a unique personality, the impress of which would be an abiding possession ...'

COBBLERS AND KINGS

> Truly, Sir, in respect of a fine workman,
> I am but, as you would say, a cobbler.
> SHAKESPEARE, *Julius Caesar*.

COBBLERS are among the humblest of men, but they have often done work which was kingly. The foundations of universal education in Britain were laid in a tiny cobbler's shop in a slum street of Portsmouth. You can see the shop today. It is preserved as one of the town's most valued sites, for there a dock-yard apprentice, crippled by a fall and turned cobbler, saved five hundred ragged children from ignorance and vice. It is a little wooden lean-to, sixteen yards by seven, with a bedroom above the shop ; and as the cobbler wrought at his bench there would be forty children or so crowded round him and his cat and his pet birds, learning to read and write, to figure and sew, to make toys and mend their shoes and clothes, and above all to value God's word and live straight lives. John Pounds—for so the cobbler was called—was one of the most gifted teachers the world has known. He evolved for himself all that Pestalozzi and Froebel were to teach us later about the natural manner of handling children. Cripple as he was, and almost penniless, he never accepted payment for his teaching, nor for curing lame children with his handmade orthopaedic boots. He fed his pupils and found them good clothes, even to special suits for chapel going on Sunday, and often took them out for a whole day's nature ramble on the hill overlooking the harbour, finding all meals from breakfast to supper. Benefactors he had for his school, but not for himself; and when one New Year morning he walked out of the schoolroom and fell dying in the house of a friend, his sole estate consisted of his shop and the pennyworth of sprats he had bought for his New Year's dinner.

Portsmouth was not slow to see the force of John Pounds' example, and his work was spread throughout Britain in a remarkable way. With great difficulty his friends had succeeded in getting painted a portrait of old John teaching as he cobbled. A print of this, with an inscription beneath, had by some process made its way into the parlour of an inn at Anstruther, Fifeshire, the birthplace of Thomas Chalmers. Dr. Guthrie of Edinburgh, while on a pilgrimage to Anstruther, saw this picture, and reading the inscription he exclaimed in astonishment to his companion: 'That man's an honour to humanity, and deserves the tallest monument ever raised within the shores of Britain.'

Dr. Guthrie himself helped to raise the monument. With the co-operation of the Earl of Shaftesbury and the warm support of Charles Dickens he founded the Ragged School Union. Although the straightforward educational work of the Union became absorbed in the national scheme of elementary education after

1870, its more specific work of caring for cripples and the destitute still continues under Royal patronage, being known as the Shaftesbury Society and *Arethusa* Training Ship ; the Fresh Air Fund is another offshoot, and commemorates John Pounds' nature rambles on Portsdown hill.

It is not a far cry from the cobbler's shop to that of the village shoemaker, who is half cobbler too. A cobbler is a man who repairs shoes by hand, and he generally works alone; the shoemaker has apprentices and employees and his shop is generally the centre of information and discussion. Shoemaking by hand is a craft which admits of conversation, of meditation and even of desultory reading, and though those local shoemakers were sometimes rough fellows who were too drunk at the week end to work on Mondays, there were among them men of culture and character. From a shoemaker's shop of the better type came Sir Henry Jones, the reformer of Welsh secondary education, who eventually occupied the Chair of Moral Philosophy in the University of Edinburgh—the highest post, perhaps, that Scottish culture has to offer. In *Old Memories* Sir Henry has painted a glowing picture of his four year's work by his father's side, in a Welsh village where every man went to Sunday School all his life. The father was a man of merry heart, who never made more than a pound a week; but his homeful of children never lacked for food or clothes or laughter, and the discussions which went on over the shoemaking gave the eager young learner the finest possible education for a boy in his teens. He learned there more live facts about human life and politics than any school can teach.

There seems to be a definite connection between shoemaking and religion, learning and philanthropy. Many of the earliest Latin missionaries of Alexandria, Asia Minor and of Gaul were shoemakers. On the second page of his *Journal* George Fox, founder of the Society of Friends, writes:

> ' I was put to a man that was a shoemaker by trade ... I never wronged any man or woman in that time ; for the Lord's power was with me, and over me, to preserve me. While I was in that service, I used in my dealings the word Verily, and it was a common saying among people that knew me "If George says Verily, there is no altering him ! " '

The power of that 'verily' became felt throughout Britain and far beyond it ; ' verily ' was the first word of the Quaker plain speech, and the suit of leather which George made for himself to go out preaching in was the earliest Quaker garb.

George Fox came from Leicestershire. From the neighbouring county of Northamptonshire came a century later another shoemaker who was destined to open a new chapter in the history of India. William Carey was the son of the village schoolmaster of Paulers Pury, near Towcester. While apprenticed to a shoemaker nine miles from his home he found a *New Testament Commentary* in his master's shop, and could not rest until he had discovered how to read the Greek in it. He was fortunate to hear of a weaver in his home village who knew Greek; the weaver had been well educated as a lad, though his dissolute ways had brought him down in the world, and with this old man he studied Greek. Carey was already an omnivorous reader, and had learnt by heart the whole of Dyche's Latin vocabulary ; his recreations were bird's nesting and the study of plants, in which latter taste he was encouraged by his uncle Peter Carey, a gardener in Paulers Pury. Thus the homely circumstances of life in a South Northamptonshire village proved a good preparation for his work in India, which brought fresh life to India's native literatures and opened new prospects for its agriculture.

In due time Carey set up for himself as a shoemaker and repairer, and gradually became known as a local preacher. He was ordained to the Ministry of the Baptist Church on August 10th, 1785, and was called to the pastorate at Moulton, a village on the road from Kettering to Northampton, with the salary of £10 a year. This modest sum he supplemented by making boots for an Army contractor, a Mr. Gotch, whose family were founders of the boot industry at Kettering, tramping to that town once a fortnight with his goods, and returning with leather. But Carey's active mind was not sufficiently exercised even by a pastorate and a business ; he kept up his wide reading ; and Cook's voyages, coupled with two publications by Johnathan Edwards of Northampton and Andrew Fuller of Kettering, set his mind working on a vast scheme for the evangelisation of the pagan world. Edwards' and Fuller's books received a great deal of attention in the county, but it was Carey who drew the positive conclusion that a solemn responsibility rested on those ' who are entrusted with the Gospel to endeavour to make it known among all nations for the obedience of faith.' This thought burned in his mind like fire ; it followed him to church and to the work-bench. He busied himself making a survey of the thought and religion of every nation, which is still of value. ' I remember,' says Fuller, 'on going into the room where he employed himself at his business, I saw hanging up against the wall a very large map, consisting of several sheets of paper pasted together by himself, on which he had drawn with a pen a place for every nation in the known world, and entered into it whatever he had met with in reading, relative to its population, religion, etc.' Thus it came about that at the meetings of the Northamptonshire Baptist Association in 1792 Carey's sermon on the theme ' Expect great things from God ; Attempt great things for God,' produced such an impression that a resolution was passed ' That against the next meeting of ministers at Kettering, a plan should be prepared for the purpose of forming a society for propagating the Gospel among the heathen.' The meeting was duly held on October 2nd, 1792, ' in Mrs. Beeby Wallis's back parlour '; the sum of £13 2s. 6d. was collected; and on June 13th, 1793, the first band of missionaries sailed for India under Carey's leadership, Andrew

Fuller and others remaining behind to ' hold the ropes.' Thus was laid the foundation-stone of the whole vast structure of modern missions.

The life of heroism, self-sacrifice and triumph which followed is too long to tell here. Carey shewed throughout his career the same patience, thoroughness and breadth of mind as he had exhibited in his tiny shop. He met with difficulties of many kinds, even with opposition from the Parliament at Westminster, where William Wilberforce pleaded his cause with great vigour. All opposition was eventually overcome by the sheer weight of his services to India. He became more proficient in Sanskrit than any other European of his day, and personally organized the translation of the Bible into over forty Oriental tongues, for many of which he compiled the first grammars and dictionaries, thus giving a new impetus to native literature in those tongues. He was made a Professor at the Government College at Fort William, and later became President, Professor of Divinity and lecturer on Botany and Zoology in the Baptist College of Serampore. Brown University of U.S.A. conferred upon him its Doctorate of Divinity, and he was admitted to the membership of the Linnean Society, of the Geological Society, and of the Horticultural Society of London. In his gardens at Serampore he carried out many experiments which were invaluable to India, though the one which pleased him most was his eventual success in growing a daisy on Indian soil. With the encouragement of Lord Hastings he founded the Agricultural and Horticultural Society of India, which is said to have formed the model for the Royal Agricultural Society of England.

Carey remained to the last the simple Christian he had been as a young man. As his long life of activity drew to its close, and other interests receded, his spirituality shone the more clearly. At the very end of his life he asked a young missionary to pray with him. As the young man rose to go, he heard a feeble voice calling him back; turning, he heard these memorable words: ' Mr. Duff, you have been speaking about Dr. Carey, Dr. Carey; when I am gone, say nothing of Dr. Carey—speak about Dr. Carey's *Saviour*.'

The thought of William Carey and Andrew Fuller leads me naturally to my own father. In the front pew in Andrew Fuller's Chapel there is to-day a brass plate recording the fact that for over forty years he worshipped in that place. My earliest memories of worship as a little boy are strangely mixed up with the memorial tablet to Fuller, which was on the wall before us. I think I learned much by spelling out the long words in it, and the phrase ' his writings were numerous and celebrated ' must have had a permanent effect on my literary style, so deep was the impression it made. Service over, I loved to tip-toe after father into the vestry, to watch the deacons piling up the collection money into neat little piles of shillings and pence, with William Carey's portrait looking benignly down upon them.

COBBLERS AND KINGS

My father, too, began his life in a village shoemaker's shop, where like Carey he learned not only to make a shoe but to study the Bible. He had no formal education, but was widely read and wrote excellent English in a fine hand ; as a speaker to country audiences and congregations he was in wide demand, for he mingled humanity and humour with a gleam of rare heavenly-mindedness. During his youth a gentleman who had become deeply interested in him offered to send my father to College if he would become a Minister of the Gospel : his reply was ' Thank you kindly, sir, but I can serve God better by making boots.' By the time I appeared on the scene he was the head of a rapidly-growing business which had spread far beyond the county, but he still retained the country tastes and the quiet insight into the loves and laughs of simple folk which he had learned as a village lad. What finer education can a boy have than to learn a craft in an atmosphere of humanity and spirituality ? Father was always as fresh as the morning, and even a lifetime of business did not lessen his keen interest in all forms of human activity. He made, I am told by experts, the very best boots in England of a certain type ; but he also made men. As a Sunday School and Bible Class teacher he set hundreds of young men on the road to success, and his employees looked up to him as a strict but just and kindly master. Like Josiah Wedgwood, he would let no piece of slovenly work pass his critical eye, and woe betide the foreman who had let it pass his ; but to the unfortunate, and even to those taken in serious crime, he was tenderness itself. His work he regarded as an art ; one of the friends of his youth became a world-renowned painter, but I truly believe that my father was an artist too. I have heard him say of a new piece of colour design in leather that it was worthy of Turner, and I know he felt it to be so. But his best and most beautiful work was done in his Bible Class, and none who heard him can forget the childlike simplicity of his spoken prayers. At the time of his passing a tradesman in the town summed him up to me in these simple words : ' He was a good man. A cobbler, but a king.'

AT HOME AND ABROAD

MASTERS OF WORDS

IN the year 1885, a Scotsman from Roxburghshire came to Oxford to devote himself entirely to his *New English Dictionary on Historical Principles*, the first part of which had been published by the Clarendon Press while he was still teaching at Mill Hill. Three years later Max Müller, Professor of Sanskrit and of Comparative Philology at Oxford, met in London a young Yorkshire dalesman who had already achieved a reputation as a philologian in Germany, and persuaded him to come to Oxford. 'You will soon be a made man, if you can keep your own counsel,' he told him, and so it proved to be. The Scotsman was Dr. (later Sir) James Augustus Murray, the principal editor of the *Oxford English Dictionary*, and the Yorkshireman Dr. Joseph Wright, who became editor and publisher of the *English Dialect Dictionary*. Both were men cast in the heroic mould; of impressive appearance, inexhaustible energy, great determination and outstanding ability; both were Northerners; both had been schoolmasters, and they both retained to the last a great love for young people, and a perennial enthusiasm for life and knowledge.

Murray worked till his seventy-eighth year on his *Dictionary* and had to leave it in the hands of his co-editors, Henry Bradley, Sir William Craigie and C. T.

Onions; Wright completed his great work with the help of his wife, financed it, superintended its publication and some years before its completion succeeded the Rt. Hon. Max Müller as Professor of Comparative Philology.

Sir James Murray was the son of a linen manufacturer. As a young man his keen interest in natural science, in languages, in dialects and in archaeology made him a notable figure in his native county, and at twenty-one he became Headmaster of the Hawick Subscription Academy. A few years later he came to London, and whilst working in the Chartered Bank of India made the acquaintance of several noted members of the London Philological Society, who were commencing the compilation of a new *English Dictionary*. In 1861 the editor-designate, Henry Coleridge, had died, and it was difficult to fill his place adequately. When all seemed black, Murray came forward with a new plan for the work and was asked to be editor. It was not, however, until 1878 that the Clarendon Press finally consented to undertake publication, and to contribute towards the expense of compilation. Meanwhile Murray had gone to Mill Hill as a master under Dr. Weymouth, the compiler of the *New Testament in Modern Speech*. While the Irishman, Edward Bowen, was setting up new standards of friendship between masters and boys and revolutionizing public school technique at Harrow, the Scotsman was doing the same thirty-nine miles away at Mill Hill.* Murray

---

*See *The History of Mill Hill School*, by N. G. Brett James, F.S.A.

made his English and Scripture lessons a centre of glowing interest ; he also threw himself into the life of the school, founding a Natural History Society and later a Museum, and putting vigour into the school debates and Magazine. In addition to all this he was toiling at the *Dictionary* in his Scriptorium, an iron building in the garden of his house, ' Sunnyside ' ; yet he would always give his time freely to boys who came in from nature rambles with new specimens. When he moved to Oxford he built a new Scriptorium and the Mill Hill one became the property of the boys. The rest of his life was filled with exacting toil for the *Dictionary*, broken only by short vacations and one voyage; but till an advanced age he kept up his cycling, his stamp-collecting, his interest in politics and in the Congregational Church. He was singularly happy in his home, his wife and eleven children all outlived him, and the success of his sons was a great joy. In 1897 Henry Bradley said at the ' Dictionary Dinner ' at Queen's College, Oxford, that it would have been ' a national calamity ' if any other than Murray had been chosen to edit the *Dictionary*, and in the short life of him published by the British Academy in 1918 Mr. Bradley wrote : ' When the remaining part of the last volume is finished, the *Oxford English Dictionary* will stand unrivalled in its completeness as a record of the history of the vocabulary of a living language, and it is to Murray more than any other man that the honour of this great achievement will belong.' Among Sir James Murray's other works two are outstanding—

his article on the English language in the *Encyclopaedia Brittanica* and his *Dialect of the Southern Counties of Scotland*, which blazed a wholly new trail in the scientific treatment of modern dialect, and was rewarded by the bestowal of an honorary LL.D. from the University of Edinburgh—the first of nine such distinctions.

During his youth Sir James had been more attracted to sciences than to languages, and the same is true of the editor of the *English Dialect Dictionary*, a work the need of which became apparent during the collection of material for the *New* (i.e. the Oxford) *English Dictionary*. The English Dialect Society, founded by Professor Skeat, set itself to collect material for a complete dictionary of dialect words in use during the last two hundred years, but an editor capable of co-ordinating the information gained was far to seek, until Joseph Wright, as yet in Germany, produced a *Grammar of the Dialect of Windhill in the County of Yorkshire*.

This book was the first to apply scientific principles to the grammar of a dialect. Its acceptance for publication by the English Dialect Society eventually led to the author, now a Ph.D. of Heidelberg, being asked to undertake the editorship of the *English Dialect Dictionary*. The work was carried out at Oxford, and the text printed by the Clarendon Press at the editor's risk, and published by subscription. Thus the two supreme works of English philology were being produced and published in Oxford at the

SIR JAMES MURRAY IN HIS OXFORD SCRIPTORIUM

JOSEPH AND ELIZABETH MARY WRIGHT
AND THEIR CHILDREN

same time, by men so well versed in the ancient languages—among Wright's publications was an *Historical Grammar of the Greek Language* (Oxford 1912)—that the University was bound to acknowledge the possibilities of work in a new sphere. These achievements undoubtedly opened the way for the recognition of Modern Languages as a subject of University study at Oxford.

Joseph Wright had been reared at Thackley, in the township of Idle, near Bradford, and he was always fond of claiming that he had been an *idle* man all his life. His father was a blaster in iron-stone quarries, a man too good-natured to work steadily, and Joseph spent a small part of his childhood in the workhouse, and the rest in a one-room cottage. But he had two great assets—a wonderful mother who remained his guide and friend till she passed away at the age of seventy-nine, and a nature naturally unselfish, pure-minded, and full of indomitable courage. He went to work at the age of six; at fifteen he was earning a man's wages as a wool-sorter, and could set his mother up in a four-roomed house, simply but adequately furnished. Before he could read and write properly himself, he had seen to the education of his younger brothers. One incident from his youth throws a flood of light on their circumstances. The family attended regularly a Primitive Methodist chapel (four attendances on Sunday for the boys, two services and two sessions of Sunday School) and on the occasion of the Prince of Wales' marriage to Princess Alexandra, the scholars had a treat. Wright always remembered that Royal wedding because he had an orange—the only one of his childhood.

The Franco-Prussian War kindled in him a desire to read the newspapers, and he set to work, learning to read from the *Bible* and *The Pilgrim's Progress*—a superb introduction to English. The task was doubly difficult, because he had never spoken, and scarcely heard, standard English, but knew only the purest Bradford dialect. He went to night schools, and educated himself in his spare time on *Cassell's Popular Educator*. Within two years he had a small night school of his own in his bedroom, and when he became famous, old scholars wrote from the farthest end of the Empire to say what an inspiration the school had been. 'The impressions I gained from you, your good mother, and humble home, has ever made you my life's hero ; and the pure gold that underlaid it all, so impressed me that I have always been thankful of the privilege I had of knowing you in all those strenuous times,' wrote a man from New South Wales in 1928.*

Wright might have been a successful and wealthy manufacturer ; he had his feet well on the first rung of the ladder ; but though he was most practical about money, it never came first with him. Throughout his life he always sought first to find the sphere in which he could render the greatest service to mankind. During a period of temporary closure of the mill at which he worked he took a post as a schoolmaster at a private

---

*The Story of Joseph Wright, by Elizabeth Mary Wright, p. 24.

school. Later he studied in Germany and France, and taught at several English schools of good quality. During this period he joined the Church of England, and was confirmed in Canterbury Cathedral; he always maintained a friendly relationship with the chapel of his youth, and in his later years was more in tune with St. Martin's-in-the-Fields than any other church, the attitude of the churches during the war having distressed him greatly. Like Sir James Murray, he was a fine teacher, and loved the work; but he could not stand parents, and seeing that this debarred him from a headmastership, he determined to leave school teaching and take a degree in Germany, where a University course was inexpensive, and he could secure enough teaching to pay for his keep. He went to Heidelberg, his purpose being to study his favourite subject, mathematics; but an invitation to attend Professor Osthoff's lectures on Comparative Philology led him into his true life-work.

At that period there were very few people in Britain who believed that a science of comparative philology could be established. Wright became convinced in Germany that it could, and while learning the essential principles of this new subject from the Germans, he brought it to a British practicality and clarity of purpose which led him to important discoveries. In particular he set himself to study the workings of sound-changes and other processes *in living English dialects*; it was this combination of wide philological knowledge and a living acquaintance with dialect which made him the one man in history who could have adequately compiled the *Dialect Dictionary*.

The sole responsibility for this great work, the index for which alone contains 99,000 references to counties and parts of counties, rested on Joseph Wright's shoulders. His savings were all sunk in it, and his reputation, as he knew, would rest upon it. Dr. John Johnson, printer to the University, who handled the production, said with justice: ' Certainly there was no other man in the world who could have done what Joseph Wright did. Elsewhere it has needed Universities to do what he did single-handed.' There was no precedent for such a work, which involved the collection of material up and down the country, largely from oral sources and tradition. Wright necessarily had a staff working under him, and helpers throughout the country who gathered material, but this great twelve-volume *Dictionary* was essentially his work.

Behind those solid volumes there lies a romance, the romance of a love so rare, so patient, so calm and deep that it sustained him throughout the task. Joseph Wright had fallen in love with one of his women students, and said no word for years. He had fostered her abilities as a philologian, and eventually had won her as his partner. In this love, even before it was declared, he had found the inspiration and courage to begin the *Dictionary*, the first part of which was published on the day of his engagement. ' It is a work that is a most sacred task to me,' he wrote to his wife before their marriage. ' Had it not been for you, nothing in the world could have induced me to undertake what seemed an impossibility to everyone else. But deep, genuine love can overcome impossibilities.'

Professor and Mrs. Wright were an ideally united couple. Their home, ' Thackley,' in North Oxford, lives in the memory of countless dons and students who found there Yorkshire hospitality and warm-hearted encouragement. There are men and women throughout the world today who could echo the quaint words of that early Yorkshire pupil, ' I have always been thankful of the privilege I had of knowing you in all those strenuous times.'

What his contemporaries thought of his work is best expressed in the words of Sir James Murray himself, the man most qualified to assess his worth, when recommending him for the Deputy-Professorship in 1891 : ' I know no one in England so fully acquainted with the science (of Comparative Philology) at present, and the problems which lie before us in the future. . . . His great strength is in the general Comparative Philology of the Indo-European languages, including especially the light which this sheds upon the form and history of the classical languages of Greece and Rome ; and it would be a great thing for the interest of classical scholarship in Oxford that this subject should be placed in his hands.' * After his passing in 1930 Sir Michael Sadler, Master of University College, wrote of him : ' He was one of the greatest English-

---

*The Life of Joseph Wright, by Elizabeth Mary Wright, Vol. I, p. 135, and Vol. II, p. 679.

men, great in character, great in humanity, great in scholarship. But the power of his will, mind and manhood inspired us all. For nearly fifty years he and I were friends, and I was always the stronger for his example.' *

The Life of Joseph Wright, by Elizabeth Mary Wright, Vol. I, Preface, p. vi. *Ibid.*, Vol. II, p. 682.

OXFORD AND MODERN LANGUAGES

THE study of modern languages made its way slowly in Oxford. It was at first no easy matter for a University so intensely devoted to the classics to see the value of such study, and until well into this century there were few if any schools which gave adequate preparation for University work of such a nature. The gradual process by which the Honour School of Modern Languages has become one of the major Schools of the University is very ably traced in the speech delivered by King Edward VIII as Prince of Wales, which is printed later in this chapter by permission of the Private Secretary. In a number of other speeches delivered as Prince of Wales the King stressed the importance of a knowledge of modern languages, and he himself set a practical example by learning to speak French, German, Spanish, Afrikaans and certain native dialects. It is probably not so well known that he played a positive part in the development of modern linguistic studies in his own University of Oxford. As an undergraduate he was one of the few men studying German, and spent part of two vacations in Germany under the guidance of his German tutor, Professor H. G. Fiedler, who accompanied him to the courts of Royal relatives, to the British Embassy in Berlin and to the Imperial Court. The War interrupted the Prince's

German studies, but after peace was signed he took an active share in the great forward move of modern language work in the University. It was he who proposed the restoration of the German Rhodes Scholarships, and he personally welcomed the first holders on their arrival. When a Mansion House Committee, presided over by the Lord Mayor, set to work to establish a Chair of Spanish in Oxford, the Prince took a keen interest. Sir Charles Bedford and Lord Nuffield supported the plan very generously, and King Alfonso XIII accepted the title of the Chair, which was approved by Decree in February, 1927. From 1927—1931 the King Alfonso XIII Chair of Spanish was held by Don Salvador de Madariaga, who resigned after the Revolution to become Spanish Ambassador at Paris and representative of Spain at Geneva.

After his visit to the Argentine, the Prince of Wales inaugurated a scheme designed to link the Universities of Buenos Aires and Oxford somewhat as the Rhodes Scholarships link Oxford with Universities in America and the Dominions. Messrs. Millington Drake of Buenos Aires and Mr. Philip Guedalla did much to support the plan, under which two graduates from Buenos Aires come each year to Oxford; it is hoped that further support will make it possible for Oxford men to go to the Argentine. Mr. Guedalla watches over the work and comfort of the visiting students, while a local committee presided over by Mr. H. R. Williamson supervises credentials and makes arrangements for entry into Colleges.

OXFORD AND MODERN LANGUAGES

In view of this lively interest in modern languages, it was natural that His Royal Highness should be invited to visit his old University to open the fine new buildings which were added to the Taylorian Institute in 1932.

The Taylor Institution, or 'the Taylor,' as it is more affectionately called in conversation, came into being as the result of a princely bequest from Sir Robert Taylor (1714—1788), a Sheriff of the City of London, who left the residue of his estate to the University to provide a building and a staff for the teaching of modern European languages. Sir Robert was a sculptor and architect of note. Two of his statues are in Westminster Abbey, and as an architect he did work of distinction at the Bank of England, at Lincolns Inn, at Clumber, and at other great houses in town and country. It is not known why he was interested in modern languages, but his own experiences as an art student in Italy, and those of his pupils abroad, may have impressed him with a sense of their value. His son, Michael Angelo Taylor, disputed the will, so that the bequest did not come to the University until 1835.

When it did come, it caused some consternation. There was genuine alarm lest the attention of undergraduates be distracted from their classical studies, and it was even proposed that post-graduate courses alone be offered.

The University, however, accepted the conditions of the bequest, and proceeded to arrange for the necessary buildings. They already had a considerable sum arising out of a legacy from Dr. Francis Randolph to be used for an art gallery, and it was decided to combine the University Galleries with the Taylor Buildings by a bold architectural design in the Grecian style. Great care was taken over the plans, and Sir Robert Smirk, the architect of the British Museum, was asked to make the final choice between those submitted. He gave a very positive decision in favour of the work of Charles Robert Cockerell, R.A., son of Samuel Pepys Cockerell, who had been a pupil of Sir Robert Taylor himself. The result was a most impressive contribution to the architecture of Oxford.

There is something singularly felicitous in the position of the Taylor Buildings. All that is finest in modern literature derives either from the study of classical antiquity, or from the liberating influence of the Holy Scriptures. Standing in the great archway which pierces the Taylor Institution, one looks either towards the portico of the University Galleries,* where the student can make direct acquaintance with the classical sculptures which so influenced Goethe and Lessing, or across St. Giles to the Martyrs' Memorial and to Balliol College, whose Master, John Wycliffe, first gave to Europe the Bible in a modern tongue. The Taylorian thus bridges the gulf between the Renaissance and the Reformation, and seems, both by its architecture and by its position, to prophesy that

---
* Now known as the Ashmolean Museum.

OXFORD AND MODERN LANGUAGES

fusion of ancient and modern culture which alone can express the highest ideals of our age.

To promote this fusion has been its function. Although its influence on undergraduate life was small until the third decade of this century, it proved from the first to be the natural channel through which the thought of modern Europe could flow to the older members of the University, who gladly recognized the great gifts of its leading Professors. Among these the Rt. Hon. Max Müller and Joseph Wright were outstanding ; between them they guided the fortunes of the Taylorian for over seventy years. The former, a brilliant and versatile scholar who was a master of the art of exposition, opened a new realm of thought to Oxford. He was in no small degree the pioneer of the Oxford we know, with its wide Imperial and international interests, and its generous acknowledgment of all that is noble in human thought.

To an Oxford still strictly Anglican and largely clerical in its atmosphere, absorbed in the study of classical and Hebrew antiquity and as yet unresponsive to the currents of world-thought, this handsome young musician and scholar, the friend of Mendelssohn and the Chevalier Bunsen, came like a breath of invigorating moorland air. Max Müller has already been mentioned in this book as the friend of John Bellows. He shared with the Cornishman the same profound sense of the divine Immanence, and the same universatility of interest in the higher aspirations of all mankind. In particular he was attracted to the thought of India, and came to Oxford in 1848 to be near the Clarendon Press, which was printing his great edition of the *Rig-veda* at the expense of the East India Company. He stayed in Oxford at the invitation of the Curators of the Taylor Institution, who eventually elected him to the Chair of Modern European Languages. So greatly did Oxford appreciate the broadening influence of his thought that it admitted him to full membership of the University without his subscribing to the Thirty-Nine Articles, and created for him a Chair of Comparative Philology, thus linking the study of ancient and modern languages, including those of the East.

Müller was keenly alive to the life of his day, and saw the immense importance to our Empire of the study of Oriental languages and culture. Few Englishmen of that period appreciated as he did the significance of our Eastern Empire, or the importance both to our Army officers and Civil Servants of a knowledge of native languages. He was rewarded by the warm-hearted appreciation of Queen Victoria, and became a Privy Councillor.

His successor in the Chair of Comparative Philology was Joseph Wright, whom he himself had discovered and brought to Oxford. When an Honour School in Modern Languages was at last established in 1903, Professor Wright not only wrote a notable series of text-books for its use, but brought the same practical acumen and business ability to bear on the problems involved in developing the new School, as he had shewn in the compilation and production of the *English Dialect Dictionary*. In this part of his work he was warmly supported by Mr. H. T. Gerrans, Fellow and Vice-Provost of Worcester College. It is impossible to do justice here to the many-sided activity of Henry Tresawna Gerrans, the ablest Oxford mathematician and one of the greatest University administrators of recent times. He was a leader in every effort to widen the influence of Oxford in other lands, and to encourage students from overseas to study in Oxford. Apart from his outstanding gifts as a mathematician, he had a wide knowledge of both ancient and modern literature, spoke German as fluently and as correctly as he did English, and was at home in a number of European countries. He was also a musician, which widened his capacity for contact with his fellow-men of every country. His marriage to Miss A. Elizabeth English of London, Ontario, brought him into contact with the culture of Canada and the United States, and his home was always open to students from the Dominions and America, as well as to those who came to Oxford from Europe, or were studying European languages. He became a Curator of the Taylor Institution, to which he gave freely of his administrative ability, and he was a Perpetual Delegate of the Clarendon Press, which has contributed so largely to the cause of modern language study by its publications. As Secretary to the Delegates of Local Examinations, and a member of the Hebdomadal Council, he was also able to do much for the general improvement of modern language work in the schools and in the University. Substantial contributions from his personal library are now in the Taylor Institution, and his memory is also perpetuated by the Gerrans Memorial Fund, the income from which is used to promote research or to enable scholars to print the results of their researches.

Mr. Gerrans was a true type of those older members of the University who made the establishment of modern language study possible in Oxford. It has only been possible here to give an account of a few outstanding men who opened new paths of thought, but a comprehensive survey of the whole history of the subject will be found in Sir Charles Firth's *Modern Languages at Oxford*, 1724—1929 (Oxford University Press, 1929), where justice is done to all who contributed to the development of this new branch of study.

A second ally of note was Professor H. G. Fiedler, who came to Oxford as the first Taylorian Professor of German Language and Literature in 1907. Professor Fiedler had already given nearly twenty years' service to British Universities, first at Glasgow and then at Birmingham, where he had become Dean of the Faculty of Arts. He was made a Member of the Victorian Order after being German Tutor to the Prince of Wales, and is still at his post after nearly thirty years. His charm as a lecturer, his kindly interest in students and his generous gifts to the Taylor Institution have earned him the deep gratitude

PROFESSOR H. G. FIEDLER, M.V.O.

THE TAYLORIAN SPEECH

of Oxford, while his beautiful *Oxford Book of German Verse* is in use throughout Britain, and has probably done more than any other one book to win the interest of young students for German literature.

The new Honour School was making steady progress under a devoted band of Lecturers when the War broke out. The rise of numbers was necessarily checked, but the War aroused the nation to the importance of a greater knowledge of Europe. After Peace was declared the School grew with great rapidity, and the need for an extension to the Taylor Buildings became urgent. As a result of this extension the School of Modern Languages is now the most compact and finely housed school in the University, with its own library, a large lecture theatre with a stage, a Senior Common room, and for each subject a Professor's study, a Seminar, and at least one lecture room. Yet growth has been so rapid that a further extension is already contemplated.

The new buildings were opened on November 9th, 1932, by H.R.H. The Prince of Wales. By a happy coincidence the Vice-Chancellor who welcomed him was Rev. F. J. Lys, the Provost of Worcester College, which had been the first College to offer an Exhibition and a Scholarship for Modern Languages.* The speeches exchanged between them are not, I believe, recorded in a permanent form elsewhere, and they

---

*Both the Exhibition and the Scholarship were won by pupils of Mr. E. W. Hallifax of Mill Hill, a Balliol man and a brilliant classical scholar, who was one of the pioneers of advanced German teaching in the Public Schools.

form a fitting end to this chapter. The Vice-Chancellor said:

'Your Royal Highness, Ladies and Gentlemen,—I have the honour of expressing the profound gratitude of the University for your Royal Highness's presence here today.

'The study of Modern Languages and Literature has become a very important part of the University curriculum. The generous benefactions which have founded new Chairs in some of these languages have been very welcome. But such benefactions as well as the increasing number of students in these subjects (an increase partly the cause and partly the effect of the foundation of the new Professorships), have made the accommodation provided by the noble endowment of Sir Robert Taylor totally insufficient.

'The Curators have for many years seen the need of expansion, and made such provision as they could for it, by wise management of their resources, by enlisting outside support, and some of them by setting an example of munificent contributions. The devoted services and generosity of the late Professor Joseph Wright, of his successor as Honorary Secretary of the Taylor Curators, Professor Fiedler, and of the late Mr. H. T. Gerrans, claim grateful acknowledgement here. In 1909, the two houses nearest the Institution were bought out of Taylorian funds; and in 1910 the next two houses by means of donations of £1,500 from Professor Wright, £1,000 from Professor Fiedler, £1,000 from Mr. Gerrans, and a loan from the University Endowment Trustees. In 1913, it was proposed to issue a public appeal for £20,000 for building and endowment. The War postponed any action, but in 1920 some additional help was got by an appeal issued by the Curators, including a further £400 from Professor Wright, £1,000 from

OXFORD AND MODERN LANGUAGES

Dr. Walter Morrison, £100 from Queen's College, and £50 from Oriel College. Even so, the present extension would not have been possible without a large donation from the Delegates for Local Examinations and without help from the University. It should, however, be remembered that the original building and its upkeep and the great work done by the Institution for many years, were financed entirely out of the Taylor endowment without imposing any burden on the University.

' To all the promoters of the Extension now happily in great part completed on plans generally approved and for which, I think, all of us feel greatly indebted to the architect, Mr. Harold Hughes, it is a cause of the greatest satisfaction that your Royal Highness has been willing and able, among the innumerable and multifarious calls of public service which incessantly find from you so ready a response, to come and open these new buildings. There are many reasons which contribute to intensify the gratification which your Royal Highness's presence affords us. We yield to none in our loyalty to your illustrious House, and in our recognition of the qualities which have made its position secure in the affections of the people when so many other thrones have been cast down. It is most fitting that this important addition to our equipment should be opened by one who is a distinguished alumnus of our University, and one who has recently shown his continued interest in it by accepting the office of Visitor of the Oxford Society. And it could not be more fittingly opened than by one who has travelled so far and seen so much of the modern world, and has shown so keen an interest in the relations of Great Britain and her commerce with other countries, and in the promotion of a fuller understanding of the mind and life and conditions of those countries with which that commerce is carried on. To that understanding, the studies of which the Taylor Institution is the home, and its great library, have made a notable contribution; and with this enlargement will be able to make that contribution still more effective. The Taylor Library is the largest collection of books relating to European languages and their literatures, mediaeval as well as modern, in the United Kingdom. It contains about 120,000 volumes, and is particularly rich in French, German, Italian and Spanish literature, in dictionaries, and literary and philological reviews. The new stack-rooms will provide accommodation for another 100,000 volumes. And we may hope, sir, that your interest in this extension may even in these difficult times encourage some of those who share that interest to emulate the great example of Sir Robert Taylor, and provide the further endowment which is needed, both for the proper upkeep and the full utilization of this new building, and also for the completion of the scheme of which it is a large part but not the whole.'

To these words His Royal Highness replied in a speech which ranks among the finest ever made on the subject of modern language study. It was listened to with keen attention by the distinguished gathering in the new Lecture Theatre of the Taylor Institution. He said :

' Mr. Vice-Chancellor,—You have spoken of my interest in modern languages, and I can assure you that, as a result of my travels in many countries, this interest has grown from year to year. I am glad to learn that the School of Modern Languages which, in my undergraduate days, was still struggling for full recognition, is now one of the larger schools in the University, and to see that in this building it has a worthy and dignified home.

OXFORD AND MODERN LANGUAGES

' It was King George I who made the earliest provision for the teaching of modern languages in the University. Before that time such instruction was provided only by a few Colleges, and I am glad to think that the first of these was my own. As early as 1581, Magdalen College appointed an Italian, Giovanni, as tutor in modern languages, who is still remembered for his excellent translation of *Montaigne's Essays*. In the preface to one of his numerous text-books he writes : " I wish there were such a law that if anyone should bring up his children without teaching them foreign languages, he should be beheaded." Much as I believe in the value of modern languages, I am not prepared to go quite so far !

' King George I, in 1724, when he drew attention to the defect that the University, being intended for a "nursery of learned men," had made no provision for the study of modern languages, decided to appoint as professor "a person of sober conversation and prudent conduct." The first holder of the Chair was a member of Christ Church. He does not seem to have been particularly well qualified for the post. Almost immediately after his appointment he took Orders, and accepted a country living, but continued to hold the professorship.

' After the death of George I, this enterprising scheme came to an end, and the professorship became a sinecure. Foreign teachers of languages, however, continued to be appointed by the University until the middle of last century. Since then the history of modern languages in Oxford has been closely bound up with that of the Taylor Institution. It owes its origin, as you know, to the far-seeing wisdom and generosity of Sir Robert Taylor, who at his death in 1788, left the bulk of his fortune to the University " for the purpose of applying the interest thereof to establishing a foundation for the teaching of modern languages." '

' Owing to certain contingencies, the bequest did not

take effect for a long time, and it was not until 1844 that the old Taylorian building was completed from designs by Cockerell, who also built the Fitzwilliam Museum at Cambridge. In the annals of your Institution, I find the names of many distinguished men, including Max Müller, Walter Pater, Swinburne and, more recently, Viscount Cave.

'In spite of the encouragement given to their study by Sir Robert Taylor's bequest, it took many years before modern languages were given a place in the examination system of the University. In 1872 French and German were added to the subjects of the Pass School, but not until 1903 was an Honour School, embracing French, German, Italian and Spanish, established. Before that time the task of the Taylorian teachers must have been very disheartening. From the evidence given before the Royal Commission of 1877 it appears that, on the average of seven years, the French teacher had a little over twelve pupils each term, the German teacher sixteen, the Spanish four and the Italian three and a half! At the first Honour Examinations in 1905 only three undergraduates presented themselves, while last June their number was 104, and I gather from Dr. Dudden's valedictory address that at present 385 undergraduates are reading modern languages.

'The Vice-Chancellor has already referred to some of the contributors to your building fund, but I should like also to mention those whose benefactions enabled the University to found a number of valuable scholarships and four professorships in modern languages.

'In 1918 Sir Basil Zaharoff gave £25,000 for the establishment of the Marshal Foch Chair of French Literature, an annual lecture and several travelling scholarships. In the same year the foundation of a Professorship of Italian was made possible by a gift of £10,000 from the late Mr. Arthur Serena. Professor

OXFORD AND MODERN LANGUAGES

Bywater and his wife left about £12,000 for a Chair of Modern Greek. The King Alfonso XIII Professorship of Spanish was created in 1927 after a Mansion House Committee, under the chairmanship of the Lord Mayor, had collected the required £25,000, to which Sir William Morris made the largest contribution. In 1919 Sir Heath Harrison gave £25,000 for travelling scholarships, and a studentship in Spanish was founded in 1920 by Don Envigae de Osma. There have also been some generous benefactions made to colleges for the promotion of modern language studies.

'Just as the School of Modern History is one of the links that join England to its past, so the School of Modern Languages is a link that joins it to the nations round us. But Oxford has forged other links by which the same service is performed. The great and far-sighted endowment of the Rhodes Foundation has served to draw our country closer to her overseas Dominions, as well as to the United States and Germany, and I have every hope that a new foundation, which bears my name, will shortly enable Oxford to strengthen our associations with the Argentine Republic. It is just a year since it was proposed to me by an Oxford and Cambridge Mission on its return from Argentina that scholarships should be provided to bring Argentines to Oxford. I heartily approved of the idea; and in the interval the money has been raised, and the University has worked out a suitable scheme, and I am happy to announce that the offer has been formally accepted by the University of Buenos Aires. I hope that Oxford has forged one more link between our country and the world in which we live.

'Much has been done in the short period since the War, but more remains to be done. The most urgent needs of this Institution are: more entrance scholarships; an endowment for the library; lectureships in

Portuguese and the Scandinavian languages; and a sum of about £15,000 to complete the extension of this building. I cannot but think that the national importance of a knowledge of modern languages will make a strong appeal, and that you will obtain the financial help you still require.

'The ever-growing intercourse between nations and the keen competition in foreign trade have already greatly increased the necessity for a better knowledge of modern tongues. It is in distribution rather than manufacture that we fall short of our competitors, and it is in the office and "on the road," rather than in the workshops, that we find it difficult to compete. We have millions of capital invested abroad, in railways, mines and other undertakings, but what is the use of sending out managers or agents who do not understand the language of the country?

'I know from my own experience what a difference it makes if you speak to the foreigner in his own tongue. Barriers seem to fall—the ice is broken. And how vital is this in diplomacy. Our national problems may be solved by English alone, but the settlement of international questions involves a knowledge of other languages besides.

'Great mistakes may be made and irreparable harm done if negotiating parties do not fully understand each other's idiom. Not every word has its exact equivalent in another language, and often a mere shade of accent or phrasing may alter the whole sense. The researcher in every other department of human knowledge cannot get on without being able to read foreign languages, for scientific and, indeed, all intellectual progress is international. If he has to wait for the translation of foreign books, he is condemned always to lag far behind— moreover, some books, and often the best, are not translated at all.

OXFORD AND MODERN LANGUAGES

' To learn a new language is to have a new life opened to us, and to know new people and modes of thought; to look at men and facts from a different point of view. The ultimate aim of teaching and learning modern languages is to give a better understanding of the life, character, ideals and aspirations of other nations. Teachers and students of modern languages may thus become emissaries of international goodwill, removing national prejudices, working for an enlightened patriotism and thus helping to promote the peace of the world. In this great work the Taylor Institution plays no mean part. I shall follow the development of your Institution with warm interest.'

THE SERVICES

THE Fighting Services have always held a high place in the favour of the Crown; the work they do is beginning to find some genuine recognition from the public. The experiences of the Great War taught most of us what it meant to be under arms, or to have near relatives in the Services; and the callous neglect of ex-service men which often distinguished earlier wars has been replaced by a large measure of intelligent care. This result was not brought about without constant and persistent work by such men as Lord Roberts and Earl Haig, Sir F. Milner and Earl Jellicoe, and by the persevering efforts of local officers of the British Legion. Much has also been done by the organization of such displays as Navy Week, the Tattoos and the Air Force Pageant, which afford the public an opportunity for contributing to Service charities, and give it some conception of Service ideals and methods.

Few but those who keep touch with the Forces realize the great changes for the better which have been carried out in the conditions of life they offer. Before the War, service to the Crown often left a man unsuited for ordinary life. Today the Services are the poor man's university. They offer to the men who enter them travel, education, technical training and abundant sport. More and more they are becoming

THE SERVICES

great Peace Forces, preparing their men to be efficient guardians of the world's peace.

This transition of ideals introduces the armed forces of Britain to a new phase of experience. At this point in their development they have found an inspiring leader in their King, who, embodying in himself the highest traditions of the serving officer, has been able as no other could do to interpret the new opportunities which this age offers. His speech before his Guards on July 16th, 1936 marks a turning point in the conception of a soldier's duty, and is in striking contrast both to the aggressive militarism found in some parts of the world today, and the pacifist idealism which, however noble, does not seem practical in our present environment. The speech in Hyde Park was a masterpiece of restrained eloquence, shot through with deep emotion as His Majesty spoke of the example of the late King George V, and again as he came to the last sentence of this paragraph:

' Only a few of us on parade this morning have known the awful weight of war, with all its horrors and yet its comradeships, during the world struggle of twenty years ago. With all my heart I hope, and indeed I pray, that never again will our age and generation be called upon to face such stern and terrible days. Humanity cries out for peace and the assurance of peace, and you will find in peace opportunities of duty and of service as noble as any that bygone battle fields can show.'

The Navy has long been regarded as a great school of character. Both King Edward VII and King George V sent their sons into the Navy because they believed it to offer the finest training for manhood. The calm and poise with which King George V steered Britain through the stormy seas of the last twenty-five years were acquired in command of destroyers and cruisers ; the King had learnt in naval service that steady devotion to duty gives man dominion over the storm. Nor is it only to the officer that the Senior Service gives a magnificent training. A public school man and University graduate who served through the war as an ordinary seaman declared that the Navy had done for him in two or three years far more than an expensive school and College education had done in fifteen. In a book* which deserved more recognition than it received, he has told the story of those years, revealing the value of the Navy as a maker of men ; and towards the close he makes a valuable proposal. Why, he asks, should the exceptional gifts of the naval instructor not be made more widely available ? Instead of breaking up our ships, why not fit them up as great floating schools with an ex-naval staff, and draft boys from city elementary schools for six months' instruction afloat under naval discipline? The instruction, which might be technical and general, would be a complete change from that given ashore, while the communal life and discipline would be invaluable to the development of character. It is a plan with immense possibilities for good, and deserves most careful consideration.

The subject of the Fighting Forces is too vast to be

---

*Three Rows of Tape by A. Trystan Edwards

THE SERVICES

dealt with here, but there is one remark which seems to sum up their character. It is said that a country receives the rulers it deserves. If this is true of the Services, and I believe it is, the characters of their leading officers are a witness to their high quality. Such men as Earl Jellicoe and Admiral Beatty, Lord Roberts, Earl Haig and Lord Allenby commanded the respect of the nation and of the world, and were as great in peace as in war. Lord Baden Powell left the Army only to build up one of the greatest peace forces humanity has ever known. That he did so was not a little due to King Edward VII, who saw the immense possibilities for good of the Scout movement, and encouraged the Chief Scout to set aside his brilliant military prospects to work for the youth of the world.

With his characteristic grasp of fundamental truths, King George V ranged the Merchant Service and Fishing Fleets among the Services by appointing the then Prince of Wales as Master. These great peace services now look to the King himself as their Master. The Fighting Services are made up of men who offer their lives to the country; and every man who goes down to the sea in ships, or does his business in great waters, goes in frequent danger of his life in peace, and in constant danger during war. In war-time the Merchant Service and Fishing Fleets provide innumerable auxiliary craft to the Navy, as well as reserves of man-power; and their daily work of transport and supply is carried on at a fearful risk. King Edward's maintenance of his Mastership of the Merchant Navy and Fishing Fleet is a grand recognition of this.

The Merchant Service requires a constant supply of highly trained officers, and, like the Navy, it has its own methods of securing them. The two famous school ships, *H.M.S. Conway* and *H.M.S. Worcester*, have a long tradition of service to the country; to them has been added in recent years the Nautical College at Pangbourne, which has given a more highly organized form to the training formerly carried out by the firm of Devitt & Moore on their ships. The *Conway* lies moored in the Mersey off Rock Ferry; the Poet Laureate was one of its cadets and has written its history. The *Worcester* lies at Greenhithe in the Thames, not far from where the old *Arethusa* had her moorings. Both ships are under the control of naval officers assisted by civilian schoolmasters, and give general as well as nautical education; a certain number of cadets pass from them each year to the Royal Navy; in the list of 'Old Worcesters' stand the names of Admiral Togo and Vice-Admiral Sir E. R. G. R. Evans, 'Evans of the *Broke*.' Their main purpose, however, is to prepare lads to be 'Liner Officers,' 'Liners' being all ships (whether cargo or passenger) which ply a regular route. The cadets wear the uniform of the Royal Naval Reserve, which many of them enter. Life on these ships, moored out in Britain's greatest estuaries, is a fit preparation for life at sea, and is full of activity and interest. I have spent very pleasant hours on both ships, especially on *H.M.S. Worcester*, and for a boy who loves a vigorous life they offer much.

THE SERVICES

As far back as 1866 Her Majesty Queen Victoria offered an annual gold medal each to the *Conway* and *Worcester*. The medal is awarded to the cadet considered by the ships' company to most exemplify the qualities which make the finest sailor. King Edward VII and King George V continued the custom, and King George granted a similar medal to the Nautical College at Pangbourne, the first medal being presented in person by King Edward VIII, as Prince of Wales. The qualities considered to make the finest sailor are enumerated as follows: cheerful submission to superiors, self-respect and independence of character, kindness and protection to the weak, readiness to forgive offence, desire to conciliate the differences of others, and, above all, fearless devotion to duty and unflinching truthfulness.

There is a certain appeal about the Fighting and Merchant Services which keeps them in the public eye. We pay the Civil Services the great compliment of taking them for granted. Their work is less spectacular, and with the solitary exception of the Income Tax Department we think little of them. The Post is as regular as the sun—a good deal more regular, thanks to our national weather. The police are guardian angels in blue, except when we have left our car too long in a congested area—on which occasions we are surprised if they are a little gruff. Robert is so calm, that we never realize how nerve-racking is the task of controlling motor traffic. An example of the strain can be seen in this: at Gloucester Cross, before the instalment of traffic lights, no officer could hold out for more than an hour.

Behind the blue-clad postmen and policemen is the vast army of men and women who wear no uniform and get no credit, upon whom the regular conduct of the country's business depends. Striking tribute has recently been paid them from an unexpected quarter; the tribunal appointed to inquire into the Budget Leakage found that no breath of suspicion rested on a single man or woman in them. When one thinks of the untold millions of money with which the Civil services constantly deal, without a complaint being raised, one realizes something of the bed-rock honesty of British character.

Those services, which involve long years of absence abroad, are peculiarly exacting in their demands on the home and personal lives of their members, and it was perhaps a delicate recognition of this which led to the inclusion in King George V's Jubilee Service of Sir Cecil Spring-Rice's noble poem *I vow to thee, my country*. This poem, written at the end of a long career of service to Britain in other lands, glows with the purest and noblest love of the homeland, a love purified by unselfed devotion until it reaches upwards to the holiest love of all.

H.M.S. WORCESTER

(W. M. Birchall, 1928)

J. Hall Thorpe

COTSWOLD HAYMAKERS

'ORDINARY FELLOWS'

GARDENERS AND COUNTRY FOLK

LOOKING back forty years or so, the people one remembers most clearly are the gardeners. They were the companions of our long days of play, and in large measure they determined our happiness.

Much of my childhood was spent playing brigand and navy games with a rather older cousin, who later became my adjutant. A great deal of our activity as brigands consisted in lying in ambush for the gardeners, and shooting at them as they bent over their work. The irony of the situation lay in the fact that our bows and arrows were made of bamboos purloined from their potting-shed. In the main they bore well with us, but the fine shades of their characters came out in their reactions.

Of Robert, the head-gardener, we lived in mortal dread. He sat enthroned in the end compartment of the long greenhouse, with three sides of glass commanding all our approaches to the potting-shed; fortunately we could, under cover of the wall, reach unseen the greenhouse furnace and there make popcorn from the hens' maize. Robert was a solid man with side whiskers, sedate, Victorian; an excellent gardener who loved his flowers and was secretly feared, I believe, even by grown-ups, when they came for plants he was loth to part with. At lunch-time—gardeners' lunch-time—Robert became approachable. There was a temporary truce, and I at least was allowed to share the bread, red cheese and bottles of cold tea, which made the most delightful meal of the day. Under these cheerful influences Robert would open out ; and as like as not he would endeavour to cry down the sea. We lived only fifty miles from the coast, but Robert had never been there. He was an orderly man, and I believe he suspected the sea of being untidy. He always stoutly maintained that it was a much over-estimated affair. ' I don't expect it's no bigger than this pond when you get there,' he used to assert.

Robert was the oldest of the gardeners, and Lenton the youngest. Lenton was dark, strong and usually genial. But there were limits to what he would stand in the way of bamboo arrows or trampled beds. Once he tethered me to a tree, and on a greater occasion he picked the adjutant-to-be and myself up by the belt, slung us over his shoulder, carried us to the pond and gave us a good ducking : a man of resource, Alfred Lenton ; today he makes the finest bowling greens in the county.

Between the two, and wholly different from either, came Bert. Bert, like the poet Clare, was the son of a Northamptonshire hedger, and though he never wrote poetry, he lived it. Joy and tenderness shone in his eyes. Every hen knew him personally, and the pony looked out for him all day. He was really the busiest of the gardeners, for he kept the poultry and stable, stoked the furnaces, and cleaned the boots till they glistened, looked after all the taps and fuses in the house, packed my father's bags when he travelled, and on occasions made an admirable footman. But Bert always had time to mend your puncture, or find you the ripe plums, or get the horse ready for an early morning ride ; and always it was done for the joy of seeing you happy. ' Why shouldn't you be happy while you can ? ' he always said ; he did not believe in putting off heaven till the hereafter. With it all he was a slight man, not so sturdy as a real labourer, and often I believe rather tired ; but he never complained or got cross, even under severe provocation.

Bert inevitably rose in the world. More and more matters were entrusted to him. From collecting rents he gradually took over the management of all our property, and, as Mr. H. Taylor, has today several plumbers and decorators working constantly under him, besides being head gardener. When my father, broken by the strain of the War years, became almost helpless, he acted as man-nurse, accompanying him to hotels and comporting himself with perfect ease in society. Like Robert Burns, he was at home everywhere, because he loved all men.

Only once did I see Bert at a disadvantage. It so happened that I was spending a holiday on Poole Harbour with my family, and that Bert brought his family down by car to Bournemouth. We had not met for years, and he drove his party over to tea with

'ORDINARY FELLOWS'

us, arriving in a Morris Isis which somewhat dwarfed our little Baby Austin. After tea we had planned a motor-boat trip, never thinking that it would be the supreme test of Bert's nerve; in fact, we had never seen him show any sign of having nerves before. He walked down the landing stage like Agag before Samuel, gazed apprehensively into the bobbing craft, and at last descended. Clinging with both hands to the seat, he submitted to being removed far from that *terra firma* where he had reigned supreme so many years. However, he soon caught the spirit of the cruise and all was well.

The country people of Mid-Gloucestershire have a character of their own. In that remarkable district which centres in Stroud, where five deep valleys radiate in to the Cotswold massif like the arms of a star-fish, town and country, agriculture and industry are inextricably mingled. The mills lie along the valley streams, their stone buildings, with bell towers and delicately moulded chimneys, looking more like monasteries than factories. On the hillsides cling the cottages of the mill hands, with their ample gardens ; on the flat uplands above men mow and reap, and the lowlands beyond the scarp are rich with pasture. Methodism found a wide response here : George Whitefield was a curate in the district and Wesley preached there time and again. The result has been a sturdy independence of character, and a blend of intellectual culture with inadaptability to the ways of the world. Men who might have been Abraham or

Joseph stride along the roads to their work. I well remember a shepherd named Thomas Wilkins Cook, a fine, bearded man with one arm missing, who worked for one master after another at the famous tithe-barn farm of Frocester Court. Cook was a fair-spoken, sturdy man and a deep thinker. With his left hand he wrote, in the early morning before work, a remarkable book originally entitled *The Good Shepherd*. It took him six years, and when it was finished he found the cost of publication to be so great that he divided it into three parts, of which one appeared under the title *Made to Fit; or A Shepherd's Inspired Thoughts How to Bring the Human World to Christ*. The book was printed by a local printer of merit, Mark Whiley, but as it had no real publisher its sale was small. It was, however, worthy of a better fate, for it revealed a remarkable understanding of the historic development of the message of salvation from the time of Abraham, and was full of passages showing acute observation of modern life and deep spirituality.

The religious teachings of the book are based on the author's every-day experiences. He says, for instance:

> 'I well remember one lambing season when it was rain and snow nearly the whole time, and I did not take my clothes off only to change my shirt for five weeks, and my boots were not unlaced from Sunday to Sunday the whole time. Perhaps some would say, you should take your boots off; if I had taken them off, my feet would swell so that I could not put them on again.

'ORDINARY FELLOWS'

Now this lasted for five weeks in succession, and I often got soaking wet and it dried on me. I could not catch cold, I had not time for that; I was worked too close to catch cold. A person never catches cold at work if he has not got a dry thread in his shirt; it is when he ceases to work that he takes cold.'

Then he draws the parallel in the life of a true pastor.

The Miltons of Mid-Gloucestershire are in fact neither mute nor wholly inglorious. I was handed today a little book of poems in a blue paper cover, for which the owner has recently refused twenty times its published price. It is entitled *Lays for the Cottage; or Rhymes for the Loom*. The author was a weaver in the mill at King's Stanley, a mile or two from Frocester, and on the title page are these lines:

> Deal gently, critics, with these lays,
> Think of the author's means and ways
>   Ere you pronounce their doom.
> By nature's grandest scenes untaught,
> Amid the shuttle's din he wrote,
> The factory was his field for thought,
>   His study was the loom.

There is a touching modesty about those lines, and had he only written 'wrought' for 'wrote' they would have been excellent.

Jephtha Young was a self-taught man of wide interests and profound religious convictions. His verses are mainly in the metres of hymns, and somewhat solemn in tone, but he could branch out when needed, as in the poem entitled *The Royal Wedding, Tuesday,*

March 10th, 1863 ; *or The Beautiful Dane*, a poem in honour of the Prince of Wales and Princess Alexandra, which swings along right manfully :

> And the bells of Old England and Scotland and Wales,
> From towers and steeples united their peals ;
> And the people were shouting in street and in lane—
> ' Long life to the Prince and the beautiful Dane.'

In eighty-four close packed pages there are poems on all manner of subjects. Jeptha Young seems to have known everyone in the district from squire to pauper, and to have understood them. He had a keen insight too into the real reasons for scarcity in war-time, and his poems on the Crimean War contain some shrewd thrusts at the profiteers. His sympathies were with the Anti-Slave States in the American Civil War, and he is as down on Parish Poor Law administrators as Dickens himself.

There is to this day a family of plumbers in King's Stanley who retain the spirit of the true village craftsmen. Thompson is their name. One of them astounded me while doing a job by bringing a copy of *The Bookman* from the kitchen, and asking if I threw such things away ? I replied that I did, knowing no one who wanted them, and the final result was that I took to calling on him once a month with my well-read copy. I found that he was not only widely read, but very musical, and had all the oratorio music stocked by his piano. The violin is his especial hobby, and he can repair a valuable instrument so perfectly that its tone is unimpaired. He and his brothers are

'ORDINARY FELLOWS'

among the few people left who are adept at making leaded windows. Only half-a-mile from him lives one of my own gardeners, Albert Cook, a solid man who owns property. Short, spare, and not over strong looking, he has never missed a morning in any weather except once when very ill, and he works all day with a dogged persistence. He has not Bert's light-heartedness to cheer him on ; children and animals he regards as interruptions, but he will leave his job to turn his hand to anything in the house—a grace rare in gardeners—and if you once get him to talk you discover unexpected depths of thought and sympathy. Once, when there was great trouble in the house, I found him waiting for me on the lawn ; he just gave me one very strong handclasp and then went on working. His was an eloquent silence.

Albert has two brothers ; one, disabled for work, keeps house for the other—and keeps it as bright as a new pin. A merry heart has Fred, and a cheerful word whenever you call. The third brother George is an untutored genius. Being short-sighted and deaf, he never rose higher than to keep the furnaces and so forth at a school, but his mind to him a kingdom is. If he can button-hole you, you are in for a searching talk on politics, or philosophy, or the sporting news of the day. For George has a well-balanced mind. Saturdays he goes to Gloucester to watch the Rugby and then has a glass of port. I am convinced he cannot see much, but he gets the atmosphere of the game, and he once startled me by coming up and remarking with great enthusiasm what a fine team Mill Hill had that year.

George is at his best at Christmas. All the family receive a gorgeous Christmas card, to purchase which he must have been saving for months, and when one takes his Christmas basket, he does the honours in his three-roomed cottage like any nobleman.

As we have said, George never rose very high in his profession. But he had the true sense of things. One evening, just as he was crossing the road to stoke his furnaces, he was run over and had both legs broken. He was hurried to hospital. When he recovered consciousness he at once asked the nurse to telephone his employer and say that the furnace fires were not stoked up for the night.

George is a gentleman of leisure now. He has been retired on a small pension, and has a cottage rent free for life. There he sits, reading to his heart's content. Peace be unto him.

SCHOOL AND COLLEGE SERVANTS

SOME of the liveliest memories which one carries away from school and college are of the domestic staff, a devoted body of men and women who receive no mention or reward except in the thoughts of those they served. First in my memories comes Signor Vesti, the School House butler at Mill Hill. Vesti was an Italian by birth, and we signalized his naturalization as an Englishman by calling him West. His dignity and ability, together with his wide knowledge of music, suited his position, and made him no unworthy attendant on Sir John McClure or on those august beings, McClure's monitors. It was West who summoned me from the masters' common room, where I was undergoing tests in Vergil and quadratic equations, and conducted me to my first call on the great Headmaster, and he made an impression on me which was just as keen twenty or so years later, when I last saw him—the impression of a man who knew his worth and his place, who rightly valued those around him, a man through whose dignity shone a great kindness.

West was a very able butler. He never lost his head, and if he sometimes looked a little flurried when our appetites were very insistent he always rose to the occasion (it is no mean matter to mess a hundred and thirty boys who may, on a dull afternoon, eat next to nothing, and after an exciting game are ready to eat their tables). He was the only man I ever knew who could successfully carry nine plates of sausages at once, and never make a faulty move.

West was in no wise limited in his interests. His knowledge of natural history was wide, and seen in a top hat on his way to the Covent Garden Opera he was a fine picture of a man. He possessed a very beautiful gramophone with what was then a considerable set of records, and on wet half-holidays he would give us splendid concerts of classical music. He took a genuine interest in each of us, and I was amazed on visiting the school fifteen years or so after leaving to find myself at once deep in conversation with him over the events of my own day. He was deeply attached to the country of his adoption, and burst into tears when he heard of the passing of King Edward VII.

If West presided over the school house, a man of different but equally striking ability ruled the bath and the changing rooms. Quartermaster Fleming, or ' Quart,' was an old Naval Quartermaster, sharp of eye and firm of voice, and he ruled his domain with a rod of iron—a rod which became strangely covered with velvet towards the end of one's last term, when his years of service were traditionally rewarded with a gold coin. One's standing with Quart was easily determined by the amount of hot water one could get out of him, for this amount varied in inverse ratio to the amount one got into with him. There were, in our day, about 250 boys in the school, and he could pick out one's towel or games-clothes simply by running his thumb down the pile from the laundry.

In addition to seeing that we did not exceed our allotted span of half an hour in the swimming bath, or use other people's towels, or scrounge hot baths, Quart conducted each week-day an hour's punishment drill on the asphalt playground. This was the only punishment given by masters at Mill Hill, and it was divided into two periods—the first of squad drill, the second of doubling steadily round the square, with idle groups watching one's agonies from the steps of the tuckshop or the Murray Scriptorium. The drill was conducted with considerable asperity, and Quart's commands could be heard a good half-mile away. A very little of his drill went a long way with the more sensitive of us, but there were hardened ruffians who seemed to regard it as their club. They spent afternoon upon afternoon looking 'straight at the back of the neck of the boy in front' of them.

My first experience of an Oxford scout was alarming. The porter of Worcester—it was Joe in those days, a mighty fellow who had every man in College sized up to a nicety, and exerted more actual authority than the Dean—took me along to the rooms on the terrace side which had been allotted to me while sitting for a scholarship. As I was taking stock of the rooms—the owner had a pretty taste in queer pipes—the door opened, and a tall, well-dressed man of handsome appearance and dignified bearing entered. I rose, thinking he was a don. ' I am your servant, sir. If

SCHOOL AND COLLEGE SERVANTS

you should want anything just open the door and call "Wyatt."' I gaped. David Copperfield before Littimer was a giant compared with me. I never dared to call 'Wyatt,' and when he poured out a tin bathful of cold water in the morning, I rose half an hour too early and splashed about in it.

I next met Wyatt on the cricket field, while I was batting for the College. I found him bowling from one end, and Johnson, the College Cook, behind the stumps. Drake, then the Senior Common-room Scout but now the Butler, was at point. Drake, I may say, had just that gentle dignity and equatorial rotundity which fits a man to be point; after fifty-five years of service to the College he has grown somewhat in circumference, and qualified as an umpire; the range of his friendships among men of the College has grown in like proportion. They were a trio of good cricketers, as well as excellent College servants. Wyatt passed away two years ago, but Johnson and Drake I still look forward to meeting when up at Oxford.

At Wycliffe the naval tradition is also strong, and many are the stories told of Chief Petty Officer Spicer, a rotund man with a round red cheery face, and a sailor's tongue. He was a man with a large family, for whose literary interests he catered by rescuing old library books condemned to the furnace. His family must have become adepts at reading novels with missing pages, for their consumption of literature was phenomenal. Mr. Spicer was a strong upholder of the

'ORDINARY FELLOWS'

library, and looked after it with a navy man's sharp eye; but whether this interest arose from gratitude for the books he received, or from dislike of too much cleaning and polishing, I never determined. As he was like other men, the motives were probably mixed.

Mr. Spicer eventually left us, and the old books have since been burnt, but he belongs still to the world-wide fellowship of Wycliffe. On a family visit to Navy Week at Portsmouth, we were threading our way through the crowd when an Eldorado ice-cream man suddenly detached himself from a barrow and tore after us. As he was very short, we could not see his face until he suddenly ducked up out of the crowd; and in a moment we were wringing hands with Mr. Spicer. Times were bad, he exclaimed, and the Admiralty had asked the Company to take on as many ex-naval men as possible. For a few minutes he was a Wycliffian again, and prosperity and good-humour shone through the lines of care on his face; then he dived back into the struggle of life. We walked on musing of the world-wide fellowship of a Public School, and on the quay at Ryde met an old School Cricket Captain on leave from China.

COUNTY MAGISTRATES

WALKING one windy morning over Minchinhampton Common with an American Rhodes scholar in his last year at Oxford, I asked my guest what had impressed him most about Britain. He replied: ' Your local administration. Your very best people give their time freely to the government of the country. With us, the better class of citizen will not be seen having anything to do with such matters. They are left to the outsiders.' That was said eight or nine years ago, and since then many of the finest Americans have realized the seriousness of the state of affairs thus described; but as far as Britain is concerned the Rhodes scholar's judgment still holds good. The freedom which we cherish as our most vital privilege is actually due to the keen interest of the better type of citizen—whatever his social class—in all that concerns the public welfare. Every normal man in Britain considers it a privilege to give some of his best time and effort to public affairs, without payment and without other reward than that of playing his part in the great whole.

On the Justices of the Peace, in town and country, rests today the responsibility for adjusting the demands of the law to the myriad problems of every-day life. Major crime may be passed to the higher courts, but the thousand-and-one matters which make life happy

'ORDINARY FELLOWS'

or unhappy are decided, not by professional lawyers, but by a bench of citizens who look on life from a normal standpoint. Today the Justices have an efficient police force to rely on; it should not be forgotten that for centuries they were the sole maintainers of law and order, especially in country districts; and that the actual working of the law depended on their administration of it. That administration was sometimes crude: Scott, in *Peveril of the Peak*, and Dickens, in *Pickwick Papers*, have made the most of that crudity; but we owe much of our freedom today to the fact that the law was made effective by men who worked and played with the people they governed.

It was not without a certain awe, therefore, that I found myself, a schoolboy of sixteen, invited to spend the summer holidays on the farm of a well-known J.P., in that southern corner of Northamptonshire, where for endless miles men grew corn, raised cattle, hunted hard and voted Tory; and, like those Warwickshire squires who people the pages of George Eliot, attended church and returned to the hospitable board and bottle.

My host was such a man as Chaucer had painted in his Frankleyn. Certainly 'it snowed in his house of meat and drink,' and more generous hospitality I never received anywhere. The house was full of activity and merry laughter, and there was enough going on the farm to keep a lad happy for months. Not all work either; some of us often slipped off with a gun and the dogs, and there were cricket matches, and the Brackley Show (with a ride on the miniature

COUNTY MAGISTRATES

railway), and such adventures as steaming down the two-mile canal tunnel at Blisworth. In the evening the house rocked to the choruses of John Peel and Annie Laurie, or the whole family would turn out to a vast game of hide-and-seek around the barns and ricks. They were ' great days and jolly days.'

Once a week, looking very solemn and dignified, our host would mount into his trap with a groom, and drive to the Bench at Towcester. He knew every poacher and drunkard in the district personally, and used to recount during the rest of the week the homely conversations in which he had tried to bring them to better ways. He was always rather stern and severe on his return from the Bench, and in later years I learned why.

Thomas Stops was a man of great independence of character. He belonged to a well-known and widely respected family, had been a churchwarden and hunted and passed the bottle with the best. Gradually, however, he began to draw conclusions of his own about life. One day he took all the wine from his cellars and poured it down the yard drain. He gave up hunting. He joined the despised Nonconformists, who, with great insight, gave him a family pew with a private door into the chapel porch. When a Nonconformist sermon became too much for him, he quietly slipped into the open air till he had recovered, and then as quietly returned. He became a Gladstonian Liberal of the most pronounced type. He was an island of dissent towards all good things in South

'ORDINARY FELLOWS'

Northants, and for ten years he lived on his farm in virtual banishment from society.

His solid qualities eventually won him a place in men's respect, but not a large place in their society. Visitors like ourselves, who shared many of his convictions, received the full benefit of this, for all the pent-up hospitality of his nature was lavished upon us. An invitation to the farm at Tiffield became, even in our generous and beautiful home, one of the events of the year; for his wife, and indeed the whole large family, gave us a never-to-be-forgotten welcome.

The tides of war eventually landed me in mid-Gloucestershire, where I came to move in a society so magistracial, if I may coin a term, that it was necessary to be very careful about one's rear lights lest one be hauled before one's colleagues, friends or family. There dawned on one the immense amount of unpaid and almost unnoticed public service put in by people of all classes in Britain, on the bench, committees and Councils, a service which renders needless the presence of hosts of officials, and keeps the life of the country sweet and wholesome.

How can anyone who knew him forget John Bramley, formerly headmaster of Queen's College, Taunton? His courtly manners and kindly wit shed a charm on common-room encounters, old people's teas, and friendly hours watching the cricket under the holm oak on the master's lawn at Wycliffe. Strict and just was John Bramley in the class-room and on the bench, a vigorous independent in church

COUNTY MAGISTRATES

meetings and a welcome sight in all society.

With him memory couples his erstwhile pupil, and eventual headmaster—for John Bramley returned to the School where he had been a housemaster, and taught classics to the upper forms. W. Arthur Sibly is one of the few men in our history who have taken over a private school and seen it grow into a full-fledged Public School with a place on the Headmasters' Conference. During a life of amazing devotion to Wycliffe College, at which he was born, and which he never left except to study at Oxford or travel, he has found time amid his multifarious activities as a Headmaster, a beekeeper, and a militant friend of animals, to do his full share in local government and on the Bench. A life-time of deciding multifarious questions of conduct among growing lads is a good preparation for the magistracy, for most men are only boys writ large. Moreover, the whole nature of life in the Stroudwater valley inclines one to an understanding of one's fellows. There are no strict divisions here between town and country, church and chapel, working and upper class. The business men are farmers in their spare time, and, the mill-hands have good gardens; and of the two brothers who for many years administered Wycliffe the one kept pedigree cattle and the other bees.

Something of the kindly atmosphere of the farm has always mellowed the scholastic atmosphere at Wycliffe. The bees, in particular, are an unmixed blessing ; they provide us all with a Christmas present of admirable honey (we do not forget to call and wish

'ORDINARY FELLOWS'

our headmaster a 'Merry Christmas,' although cones of honey are not always easy to carry away without casualties) and the severity of class work is not infrequently interrupted by an harassed secretary rushing in to say that the bees are swarming.

One more figure rises in the memory: Alderman James Clegg Kimmins of Stonehouse, Gloucestershire, has just passed to rest after sixty-five years of continuous public service. From 1871, when he was made an overseer of his parish, until his passing in April, 1936, he always held one or more administrative posts.

When he was yet a young man the sudden loss of his father threw upon him a heavy burden. He would work for twelve hours a day in a flour-mill, and return home to study natural science with other members of his family, who started a school to supplement their resources. Of that little group, a brother became a doctor of science, a master at The Leys, and later, Chief Inspector of Schools to the L.C.C., while a sister went to India and founded the Girls' High School at Panchgani, of which she was also Principal. James Kimmins taught science in the evenings at the home school, and the wide contact with education which his experience brought him was invaluable to Gloucestershire. With the passing of the Education Act of 1902, and the transference of educational control to the counties, he entered on a wide sphere of service. From the first he was a member of the County Education Committee, of which he subsequently became chairman; he was elected to the Higher Education

COUNTY MAGISTRATES

Committee, represented the county on the Council of Bristol University, and gave much valuable evidence before the Burnham Committee. He was also a member of the Stroud Educational Foundation. In all he gave thirty-four years' service to Gloucestershire in this one sphere.

This was enough for any one man who had his own business to manage and a large family who sought and always found his keen and alert interest in all their affairs, but James Kimmins' capacity for service seemed unlimited. In 1888 he had been elected a member of the Board of Guardians for the district. The meetings of the Board were not open then to the press, and he at once proposed that they should be. The resolution was defeated by forty-two votes to three. 'Gentlemen,' he said when the result was evident, 'you can exclude the press, but you cannot exclude me.' From that date he himself reported the meetings with unwelcome candour; within six months he had won his point and the press was admitted. By such acts of vigilance are our liberties maintained.

When County Councils were created in 1889, James Kimmins was elected at once for his division, and served for nearly half a century; he was created an Alderman in 1922. From 1904 onwards he was a Justice of the Peace and a member of the Stroud Rural District Council. During the war he added to these offices the arduous tasks of Chairman of the County Appeal Tribunal and later of the War Pensions Committee. He is also notable as having been the only

'ORDINARY FELLOWS'

man in British constitutional history to fulfil all the duties of a parish council singlehanded for over two years. Owing to strong opposition to County schemes, the Parish Council of Cainscross resigned in 1914 and the County Council nominated him to fulfil their duties. When the time for electing a new Council came, no nominations were sent in, and Mr. Kimmins continued to transact all business until 1916. It is an interesting coincidence that Cainscross had come to have its own Parish Council as the result of a plan devised and carried through by him in his early days as a County Councillor.

James Kimmins was a modest and retiring man, who preferred a book by the fire or a walk with a gun to society life. He was amazingly alive to all the variations of public affairs at home and abroad. These often caused him grave anxiety, but he never lost his poise, or showed any sign of disturbance.

Once, and once only, did he receive a great popular ovation. When the crisis of 1931 came, he was one of the oldest Liberals in the mid-Gloucestershire division; it was he who nominated the Conservative Nationalist candidate, and when he stepped on to the platform at the great mass meeting in Stroud, the whole assembly rose to its feet and cheered till the roof shook. On those great political occasions one had only to look at him to see how apt a symbol of Britain is the lion. The lion is nominally a gentle creature, with a calm dignity in repose; when roused to battle it is the embodiment of courage and majesty.

INTERLUDE
THE SCHOOL IN THE WEST
A Song of Wycliffe

We come from the East and the South and the North,
From the Tees' side and Dee's side and Wales,
From the fair Midland, and the Cornish Strand,
From the Severn's roll and Thames' quiet vales;
To the West,
To the West,
To the homely heart of England in the West,
To the School's
Gentle rule
In the valley deep and cool,
To the School we love the best.

We come from the North and the East and the South,
From the prairie and bushland and veldt,
From Ceylon's fair isle, and the banks of Nile,
From China and the Indies and the Belt;
To the West,
To the West,
To the Mother-heart of England in the West,
To the School's
Gentle rule
In the valley deep and cool,
To the School we love the best.

We work and we play and we laugh and we sing,
And we wander o'er upland and vale,
To where Tyndale grew, e'er our land he drew
To the Bible's ever fresh and wondrous tale.
From the West,
From the West,
From the golden heart of England in the West,
Came the calm and stately roll
Of the Scripture's mighty scroll,
From the land we love the best.

We read and we dream and we hope and we pray,
For the thoughts of boyhood wander far and wide,
And we ponder deep as we sink to sleep
Of the life that lies before us with our Guide,
When the School's
Gentle rule,
Will relax in youth and manhood's surging sea,
And we'll gaze
Through the haze
At those golden sunny days,
In the School we'd love to see.

THE ENGLISHMAN—LOVER OF FLOWERS

HENRI TAINE, in that sparkling *History of English Literature* of his, so rich with rare pictures of the national life from age to age, has declared that the Anglo-Saxon found within himself a natural affinity with the Hebrew Scriptures. The observant Frenchman has dwelt on a common fund of moral earnestness, of deep searching of the heart which unites the Hebrew and Saxon stock ; he has remarked less a common love of trees and flowers. The cedar of Lebanon was to the Israelite what the oak is to the Englishman—the symbol of abiding strength; and the rose of Sharon had a place in the heart of psalmist and prophet only equalled by that given to the English rose. From Geoffrey Chaucer in the fourteenth century, kneeling in ecstasy over the early spring daisy, to Kingsley Fairbridge, in the twentieth, pouring out his joy at first seeing the same flower after a life-time on the brown African veldt, Englishmen of the most varied types have proclaimed their reverent love for all ' the lilies of the field.'

Frederich Oakes Sylvester of St. Louis has told us his love of

> the man who goes
> Not songless to the common tasks of life,
> But twines a flower round his tools of trade ;

he could have found such men all about him in

England. Go where they are building a house of Cotswold stone, and you will see the mason lay a flower on the centre of the lintel he is carving. Come where a regiment of soldiers has pitched camp for a week's training; within twenty-four hours there is a garden round the sergeant's quarters. Burrow into the heart of a great industrial city, and you will understand Stanley Baldwin when he says 'Nothing can be more touching than to see how the working man and woman after generations in the towns will have their tiny bit of garden if they can, will go to gardens if they can, to look at something they have never seen as children, but which their ancestors knew and loved. The love of these things is innate and inherent in our people.' He is only repeating what Cowper wrote a hundred and fifty years earlier in *The Task*.

This love of flowers pervades all ranks of the people. There is one pleasure which the Englishman does not take sadly, and that is his garden. The shrewd and analytical Lord Bacon expands in his essay *On Gardens*. The combative Andrew Marvell could turn aside in the very midst of the Civil War to brood on Lord Fairfax's lawns

> Annihilating all that's made
> To a green thought in a green shade.

Nor does the Englishman of today yield a point to his ancestors. It is said of a certain pioneer of industry that he was rarely seen without a beautiful red rose in his button-hole; and who does not know the

INTERLUDE

distinguished family of statesmen who for two generations wore an orchid in the House of Commons?

But it is the poets who have borne richest tributes to our love of flowers. Does Spenser wish to celebrate a betrothal? He walks by 'Sweet Thames' and sees a flock of nymphs—

> And each one had a little wicker basket
>   Made of fine twigs, entrailéd curiously,
> In which they gather'd flowers to fill their flasket,
>   And with fine fingers cropt full feateously
>   The tender stalks on high.
> Of every sort which in that meadow grew
> They gathered some; the violet, pallid blue,
>   The little daisy that at evening closes,
> The virgin lily and the primrose true,
>   With store of vermeil roses,
>   To deck their bridegroom's posies.

Even such homage does Milton in sombre mood beg of the vales for his young Lycidas, bidding them:

>   hither cast
>   Their bells and flowerets of a thousand hues;

and he lingers over this offering:

> Bring the rathe primrose that forsaken dies,
> The tufted crow-toe, and pale jessamine,
> The white pink, and the pansy freaked with jet,
> The glowing violet,
> The musk-rose, and the well-attired woodbine,
> With cowslips wan that hang the pensive head,
> And every flower that sad embroidery wears;
> Bid amarantus all his beauty shed,
> And daffadillies fill their cups with tears.

THE ENGLISHMAN, LOVER OF FLOWERS

This wealth of beauty lifts his thought from mourning to joy and gratitude for Life Everlasting.

To Shakespeare, flowers were a necessity of existence. Titania must needs sleep on

> a bank where the wild thyme blows,
> Where ox-lips and the nodding violet grows ;
> Quite over-canopied with luscious woodbine,
> With sweet musk-roses and with eglantine

and so the pageant of flowers links poet to poet and age to age, shining through the deep musings of Keats, cheering the distraught glooms of Shelley, softening Wordsworth's heart in hard cities, calling to Matthew Arnold from Bablock's ferry, whispering to Rupert Brooke in far countries, luring even the realist Kipling to express the unity of our far-flung Commonwealth in a song of flowers calling to men from each Dominion in turn :

> Buy my English posies !
> Kent and Surrey may—
> Violets of the Undercliff
> Wet with Channel spray ;
> Cowslips from a Devon combe—
> Midland furze afire—
> Buy my English posies,
> And I'll sell your heart's desire !

THE THREE NATIONS

THE HEART OF SCOTLAND

THE Scot loves his country with a passionate devotion, yet he often finds his richest opportunities outside its borders. Scotland has the supreme gift of being able to give ; her best is poured into the common treasury of the Empire, and, in men like Livingstone, is given freely for the good of all mankind.

Burns will always remain the Scotsman's poet, but the four great men of letters who have succeeded him belong to us all. Sir Walter Scott, Carlyle, Robert Louis Stevenson and Barrie are Scotland's gift to all who speak the English tongue. Diverse as are their talents, they are alike in a certain bedrock purity and manliness which pulse through all their being. Carlyle is indeed the prophet among them, and a certain sombre dourness hangs like a mist around his thought; but the other three shine like the sun with the joy of living. No story by Scott, however harrowing may be the scenes described, leaves one with a sense of sadness; the inherent nobility and sunniness of his loving heart irradiate the pages. Robert Louis and Barrie have the supreme gift of understanding childhood—a final test which even Shakespeare never passed. Take Scott, Barrie and Stevenson out of modern literature, and how much of the sunshine is gone !

THE THREE NATIONS

We have already been reading in this book of the many-sided contribution of Scotsmen and Scotland to our national life. Go through the pages and assess it. Our Royal Family are never happier than when they are in Scotland, and two of the present Princes have taken Scottish brides. Sir Alfred Yarrow found the fullest opportunity for the development of his great gifts on the Clyde, and Glasgow placed him on the roll of her Doctors of Law. In the realm of education and scholarship we have read of the great contributions made by Sir John McClure and Sir James Murray. Dr. Guthrie heads the movement for the Ragged School Union, and Professor Blackie is one of the foremost to appreciate and encourage John Bellows at his dictionary and Sidney Dobell in his poetry.

On a sterner field and amid sadder scenes the character of Field-Marshal Sir Douglas Haig stands out in rugged grandeur. It was the essential Scotsman in him which brought his armies through—the hardihood, the immense capacity for work, the profound, bedrock honesty, the deep piety of his character. The conviction that he was called of God to his task sustained him in those awful days of March, 1918, and at the height of the German advance he found time to attend divine service each morning. The spirit of the old Covenanters was upon him. No grander passage ever flowed from British pen than his message on Thursday, 11th April, 1918 : 'To/All ranks of the British Force in France.'

THE HEART OF SCOTLAND

In this message Haig gave unstinted praise to all ranks of the Army for their splendid resistance under the most trying circumstances, and reminded the weary that victory would lie with the side which held out the longest. Finally there came the appeal to fight it out to the end ' with our backs to the wall.' The greatest thing about this appeal was Haig's deletion of the last sentence, which can still be read in the manuscript. It ran: ' Be of good cheer, the British Empire must win in the end.' That was a natural thing to write in such a moment, but the deep thinker in Haig must have seen that these words did not stand the test of truth, and he left the appeal to rest on surer ground, closing it with the words ' The safety of our Homes and the Freedom of mankind alike depend upon the conduct of each one of us at this critical moment.'

Scotland is a land of the warrior and the wanderer, of those who go forth to battle or to toil in other lands. In her heart there is a noble sorrow. Her national music is the bagpipes' wail, a sound so sad and sweet as to be heart-rending. The Scotch are a reserved race, but when the pipes play they forget their reserve, and the sound of them in an alien land can call forth a passionate sigh for home. They express their sorrow in music, in poetry and in art, a sorrow which ennobles and purifies, for it rises beyond mere mourning to a sense of the glory of sacrifice. That is why the Scots have raised such a superb memorial to those who fell in the Great War. The Scottish

THE THREE NATIONS

National War Shrine at Edinburgh is a supreme work of art, an expression in stone and glass and bronze of the very heart of Scotland, its sadness, its nobility, its pride in suffering, its glory in giving all.

THE SCOTTISH NATIONAL WAR SHRINE: THE CASKET PRESENTED BY
KING GEORGE V AND QUEEN MARY

KING GEORGE V AND QUEEN MARY LEAVING THE NATIONAL MUSEUM OF WALES, 21st APRIL, 1927

THE HEART OF WALES

'TO teach the world about Wales, and the Welsh people about their own Fatherland'—this epigrammatic phrase happily expresses the purpose of ' Yr Amgueddfa Genedlaethol Cymru ' (The National Museum of Wales).

The museum is one of the most beautiful buildings in Britain, and its beauty is enhanced by the setting. Turning out of Queen Street, Cardiff, under the walls of Lord Bute's castle, one comes after a few moment's walk into Cathays Park, a wide, well-treed expanse crossed by spacious boulevards. On the left the surrounding walls of the castle tower above the moat ; at right angles to the walls lie three magnificent buildings in white Portland stone, the Courts of Justice, the City Hall and the National Museum. In the space in front of these stands the equestrian statue of Lord Tredegar, who led the charge of the Light Brigade at Balaclava, and the South African War Memorial of Wales. Behind the three buildings the National War Memorial gleams white in the middle of a spacious lawn, around which are grouped other white stone buildings—the University College of South Wales, the County Hall and the Technical College. The whole makes a national and civic centre only to be equalled by the surroundings of St. James's Park, Westminster, and the heart of Edinburgh.

The museum is the result of a long, sustained effort by the Welsh people to express the genius and culture of their race and the essential qualities of their country. The City Museum of Cardiff furnished the nucleus of the collection. King Edward VII granted a charter for a National Museum in 1907. Five years later King George V laid the foundation-stone. Owing to the Great War and the economic difficulties which followed, it was nearly fifteen years before, in company with Queen Mary, the King formally opened the part of the museum then completed. Since that time Prince George has opened another wing, which includes the beautiful Reardon Smith Lecture Theatre.

The impression which the visitor receives as he approaches the museum and passes into the entrance hall through the great bronze doors is one almost of gladness. The architect has made use of space, height and material to give a wonderful sense of freedom, and the museum authorities have enhanced this by placing only a small number of exhibits of great beauty and interest in this hall, which is used to epitomize the contents of the whole museum. Of especial interest are the groups of statuary, many of them by Sir Goscombe John, R.A., of Cardiff, and the robes, crown and insignia used by King Edward VIII at his Investiture as Prince of Wales.

The exhibits in the galleries are so arranged as to give a broad outline of the art, culture and industries, fauna, flora and geology of Wales at different periods, without wearying the visitor. The student who

THE HEART OF WALES

requires more has only to apply to the Keeper of a Department to be made free of the extensive reserve exhibits, fully card-catalogued, which he can handle as he requires, taking photographs or examining specimens under a microscope. There is a large staff of experts whose services are always available to the public at the museum, and who travel about Wales giving lectures and assisting in co-ordinating the work of other museums in the country, or searching for new exhibits. A good deal of field work is also done by the staff, whose researches are embodied in publications. The museum is, in fact, a cultural centre for the nation.

It is not easy to capture the spirit of a country so austere and mountainous, inhabited by a people so richly endowed with poetic and religious imagination. Nothing exhibited in a building can give back the atmosphere of her little hillside chapels, or echo the music of the shepherd's song on the lonely mountainsides. It is easier to represent South Wales, its coalfields and busy ports. Yet, in so short a time, a very wonderful collection has been made in the Museum, although only two sides of the quadrangle are as yet completed. The observant visitor receives a strong impression that the Welsh nation, proud of its culture and history, has endeavoured to make these known to the world in a singularly gracious and beautiful way. An hour at the National Museum of Wales is an hour of refreshment and inspiration. One leaves feeling that one has been admitted as a valued guest into the heart of Wales.

THE HEART OF ENGLAND

A LONDON professor once startled me by referring to Lancashire as 'The Heart of England.' Though of a family long connected with that vigorous county, I could not subscribe to the judgment. The heart of England is a big one; it cannot be confined in any one locality. Stanley Baldwin would find it in Worcestershire; a Shakespeare, perhaps, in Warwick. Dickens felt nearest to it in Kent—unless, indeed, one might say that to him London was England. Westminster belongs to the Empire, but there are strong claims for the rights of Piccadilly Circus or Trafalgar Square to the title. Yet no-one who knows his Gloucestershire will doubt that in this land of Cotswold hill and Severn plain he is very near the heart of England.

In Gloucestershire one is in touch with almost everything that is English, from the *Domesday Book* to W. G. Grace and Hammond. The two greatest English rivers are here within a few miles of each other, and are joined by a canal which runs hard by the tombstone at Stonehouse on which George Whitefield preached the first open-air sermon of the Wesleyan revival, and, a few miles further, passes the village of Brimscombe where Roger Bacon went to school. One may stand on the Cotswold scarp, close to the childhood home of William Tyndale, and only a few miles from the house where he formed the resolution to ' cause a boy that driveth the plough to know more of the Bible ' than the country clergy of that day. One wonders if it is not in part the gentle beauty of Gloucestershire which shines through every page of his translation. For certainly it is right that a Gloucestershire man should have brought forth the book which was to maintain for all time the unity of the English language, for the folk of Cotswold and Severn plain have preserved the simplicity and calm of the Anglo-Saxon nature. They are not swept by the tragic emotions of Hardy's Wessex countrymen, nor bewildered by the superstitions of the bleak Western moors ; continental influence has penetrated but little here, and the rough energy of the North is unknown.

From Haresfield Beacon, rescued at the last possible moment from the builder and given to the nation, one may gaze over Western Britain from Exmoor to the Malvern Hills, from the Cotswolds to the Black Mountains in Wales, and see wide stretches of the Bristol Channel. In the near distance are the docks of Sharpness, where ocean-going liners are unloading into barges which go by Ship Canal to Gloucester, the *Caergloui* of the Britains and the Roman *Glevum*. The streets of Gloucester are still those of *Glevum*, and John Bellows once took a party from the Royal Archaeological Institute round the city, pointing out from a plan the marks of Roman occupation ; at the last moment he told the party that the plan was one, not of *Glevum*, but of Ancient Rome—so remarkable was the uniformity of town planning in the Roman Empire. In earlier ages Gloucester was the frequent abode of the ruling monarch; in the Chapter House William I ordered the creation of the *Domesday Book*; his brother Robert of Normandy and Edward II are buried in the Cathedral. Along the line of the scarp may be seen fortress after fortress of Briton and Roman, that at Painswick rising to a thousand feet above the sea. Up the broad plain between the Severn and the Cotswolds Henry Bolingbroke rode to seize a crown, and Margaret of Anjou to lose one. The stately manors and farms, built and tiled with stone from the hills, recall the fact that this was the great wool-farm of England, and that in slightly later times the port of Bristol, open to new-found America, was a source of great prosperity to the county. Northward, the Forest of Dean bulks against the skyline, rich with the more modern wealth of coal.

The districts round Tewkesbury and Minchinhampton are known wherever the English language is read; they are the country of *John Halifax, Gentleman*. Perhaps no book so faithfully presents the fundamental ideals of the English middle-classes; certainly none is more widely loved. Tewkesbury is Norton Bury; the home of Abel Fletcher and the house of the fourteen windows, the alley where John first saw Phineas and the grey Abbey Church are much as John Halifax knew them; even the great yew hedge is there. It was to Cheltenham that John and Phineas went to see

Sarah Siddons and 'Mr. Charles' in *Macbeth*, and Longfield House is Detmore House at Charlton Kings, the home of the Dobells, where Dinah Muloch was staying when John Dobell took her to visit Tewkesbury, and, sheltering in an alley from the rain, she saw a child from Tudor House give a slice of bread to a beggar : that incident gave the first inspiration for her famous book.

But it is round Minchinhampton Common that memories of John Halifax cluster most thickly. The Common is Enderley Flat, 'the highest upland in England,' a source of constant joy to all who know it. Close under its edge stands Rose Cottage; and in the valley is John Halifax's mill. At Rose Cottage the book was written, and probably Sydney Dobell wrote there these lines from *Balder* which make him almost Shakespeare's peer :

> This dear English land !
> This happy England, loud with brooks and birds,
> Shining with harvests, cool with dewy trees
> And bloomed from hill to dell; but whose best flowers
> Are daughters, and Ophelia still more fair
> Than any rose she weaves; whose noblest floods
> The pulsing torrent of a nation's heart;
> Whose forests stronger than her native oaks
> Are living men; and whose unfathomed lakes
> For ever calm the unforgotten dead.
> In quiet graveyards willowed seemly round,
> O'er which Today bends sad, and sees his face.
> Whose rocks are rights, consolidate of old
> Through unremembered years, around whose base

THE THREE NATIONS

The ever-surging peoples roll and roar
Perpetual, as around her cliffs the seas
That only wash them whiter ; and whose mountains
Souls that from this mere footing of the earth
Lift their great virtues thro' all clouds of Fate
Up to the very heavens, and make them rise
To keep the gods above us !

INDEX

Admiralty, 18, 20, 24, 158
Africa, 79-82
Air Force, 138
Alexandra, Queen (also as Princess), 25, 115, 151
Alfonso XIII, King, facing 25, 122, 135
Allenby, Lord, 141
d'Alton, Count, 33
America (U.S.), relations with, 7, 17, 41, 87-9, 92-4, 135
Ampthill, Lord and Lady, 78
Arethusa, The, 103, 142
Argentine, 23, 122, 135
Army, The, 6, 9, 126, 138-9, 141
Arnold, Matthew, 35, 171
Arnold, Dr. T., 43
Atchley, R. W., 68
Australian XI, 64

Bacon, Lord, 169
Bacon, Roger, 180
Baden-Powell, Lord, 56, 141
Baldwin, Stanley, 56, 169, 180
Balliol College, 124, 129
Barnett, C., 67
Barrie, Sir J., 173
Beaconsfield, Lord, 21
Beattie, Lord, 141
Bedford, Sir Ch., 122
Beith, Ian Hay, 54
Belgians, King of, 27, 81
Bellows, John, 91-100, 125, 174
Bellows, Mrs., 93-4   [181
Bellows, J. E., 99

Bellows, Philip, 98
Bentley, Thomas, 13, 14, 15
Bible, The, 90, 96, 107, 109, 116, 124, 167-8, 181
Bigland, P., 99
Blackie, J. S., 92, 174
Blyth, Hon. Ivo (Lord Darnley), 73
Board, 68
Bonaparte, Lucien, 91
Bonaparte, Napoleon, 39
Bowen, Rev. C., 33
Bowen, Edward. 33-40, 63, 112
Bowen, Lord, 33
Booth, Gen. W., 76
Boy Scouts, xvi, 7, 141
Bradley, Henry, 111, 113
Bramley, John, 162-3
Brearley, W., 64
Britannia, xiv, xvi, 60
British Academy, 113
British Association, 28, 31
British Commonwealth (or Empire), 1, 2, 4, 7, 9, 63, 126, 135, 171, 175, 180
British Legion, 138
Brooke, Rupert, 171
Brontë, Charlotte, 86
Browning, R., 86
Bunsen, Chevalier, 125
Burns, Robert, 173
Burroughes, Miss, 76
Bute, Lord, 177
Butler, Dr. H. M., 34
Buxton, Alfred, 81

185

INDEX

Byron, Lord, 36, 85
Bywater, Professor, 135

Cadbury (family), 41
'Cambridge Seven,' 74
Campbell-Bannerman,
  Rt. Hon. Sir H., 48
Campbell, T., 83
Canada, 6, 127
Carlyle, T., 86, 173
Cardus, N., 63
Carey, W., 104-8
Carey, P., 105
Cave, Viscount, 134
Chalmers, T., 102
Charlotte, Queen, 13
Chaucer, G., 88, 160, 168
Chesterton, G. K., 65
China, 24, 73-78, 158
Chivers (family), 41
Christchurch College, Oxford, 133
Christ Jesus (under various titles), 5, 57, 74, 79, 80
Civil Service, 126, 143-4
Clare, John, 146
Clarendon Press, 111, 112, 114, 126-8
Clarkson, T., 17
Cockerell, C. R., 124, 134
Cockerell, S. P., 124
Colenso, Bishop, 38
Coleridge, Henry, 112
Congo, 25
Conway, H.M.S., 142-3
Cook, A., G. and F., 152-3
Cook, Captain, 105
Cook, T. W., 149-150
Cowes Week, xvi, 25, 59-62
Cowper, W., 94, 169
Cox (Sussex), 68
Craik, Mrs. (Dinah Muloch), 183
Craigie, Sir W., 111
Crush, Wm., 27

Curzon, Lord, 78

Darwin, Charles, 16
David, King, 5, 21
Denton, J. S. and W. H., 66-7
Denton, D., 67
Devitt & Moore Ltd., 142
Dickens, Charles, 102, 160, 180
Divine, Man's relation to the, 5, 35, 44-5, 51-2, 56, 71-82, 84, 89, 92, 95-7, 99, 125
Dobell, Clarence, 86
Dobell, John, 83, 85
Dobell, Sydney, 83-90, 95, 174, 183
Dobell, Mrs. Sydney, 85, 95
Domesday Book, 182
Dolly Vardon, 61
Drake, Sir Francis, 36, 37
Drake, W., 157
Drake, Millington, Messrs., 122
Drummond, Henry, 4
Ducie, Lord, 91, 95, 99
Dudden, Dr., 134
Duff, Rev., 108
Duleepsinhji, K. S., 69

Edward II, 182
Edward VII (also as Prince of Wales), vii, 19, 25, 98-9, 115, 139, 141, 143, 151, 155, 178
Edward VIII (also as Prince of Wales), vii, ix, xvi, 6-10, 42 (Royal visitor), 121-3, 129-137, 139, 143, 178
Edwards, A. T., 140
Edwards, Johnathan, 105-6
Eliot, George, 160
Elizabeth, Queen, 37
Emerson, R. W., 95
English, Miss A. E., 127
Eton College, 42, 56
Europe, 15, 16
Evans, Sir E. R. G. R., 142
Fairbridge, Kingsley, 168

186

INDEX

Fairfax, Lord, 169
Faith-healing, 76-7, 80
Faraday, Professor, 19, 28
Farmer, John, 34-39
Faulkner, Sir A. B., 83
Fiedler, Professor H. G., 9, 121, 128-130
Firth, Sir C., 128
Fisher, Lord, 20, 25, 30
Fishing Fleet, 6, 141
Fleming, Qmr., 155-6
Fox, George, 104
France, 8, 9, 20, 24, 38, 88, 117
Friends, Society of, 97-9, 104
Froebel, F. W. A., 101
Fry, C. B., 64
Fry (family), 41
Fuller, Andrew, 105-108

George I, 133
George V (under various titles) vii, xv, 1-5, 7, 20, 27, 30, 59-62, 98, 139-140, 143-4, 178
George, Prince (D. of Kent), 178
Germany, 2, 9, 10, 11, 14, 38, 111, 117, 121-2, 127, 135
Gerrans, H. T., 127-8, 130
Gilbert, W. S., 37, 43
Giovanni, 133
Girton College, 28, 31
Gladstone, Rt. Hon. W. E., 11, 47
Goethe, J. W. von, 11, 12, 14, 124
Gordon, General, 25
Gotch, Mr., 105
Grace, W. G., 64, 67, 180
Grenfell, Sir Wilfrid (William), 73
Grubb, N. P., 80
Grunne, Count F. de, 81
Guedalla, Philip, 122
Guthrie, Dr., 102, 174
Haig, Earl, 138, 174-5

Hallifax, E. W., 129
Halpin, Col., 23
Hammond, W., 67, 180
Hardy, Thomas, 181
Harley, Rev. R., 47
Harris, N. E. P., 68
Harrison, Sir H., 135
Harrow School, 33-40, 42, 112
Hartland, Dr. E. S., 99-100
Hartley (family), 41
Hastings, Lord, 107
Hawick Academy, 112
Hedley, Mr., 23
Henry Bolingbroke, 182
Hilditch, J., 22, 23
Hill, Miss, 52
Hoar, Senator, 92, 95
Holmes, O. W. (author), 92-5
Holmes, O. W. (Chief Justice), 92
Hübner, Dr., 91
Hughes, Harold, 131
Hughes, Thomas, 47
Hunt, Holman, 86

India, 3, 69, 74, 78, 104, 106-8, 125-6, 164
Italy, 9, 14, 24, 85, 88
International Friendship, 2-4, 9, 131-2, 136-7

Jaques, R. (Robert), 145-6
James, N. G. B., 48, 112
Jellicoe, Lord, 30, 138
Jessop, G. L., 64
John, Sir Goscombe, 178
Johnson, F. J., 157
Johnson, Dr. John, 118
Johnstone, Miss Marion (see McClure, Lady)
Jones, Sir Henry, 103

Keats, John, 171
Kemp, Caleb, 98

187

INDEX

Kerr, Miss, 76
Khartoum, Relief of, 25
Kimmins, J. C. C., 164-6
Kimmins, Dr. C., 164
Kimmins, Emily, 164
Kings College, London 33
Kingswood School, 68-9
Kipling, Rudyard, 171
Kitchener, Lord, 78
Knott, A. G., 68
Kumm, Dr. K., 79

Lenton, A., 146
Lessing, G. E., 124
Leys School, 164
Lincoln, Abraham, 2
Lindo, Esther (see Mrs. Yarrow)
Livingstone, D., 173
Lorimer, Sir Robert, xvi
Lyon, John, 37
Lys, Rev. F. J., xvi, 129-132
Lyttelton (brothers), 70
Lyttelton, Hon. E. (as Headmaster of Eton), 56

Macdonald, George, 86
MacLaren, A. J., 64
McClure, Sir J., 41-53, 154, 174
McClure, Lady, 43, 45
Madariaga, Don S. de, 122
Magdalen College, Oxford, 133
Margaret of Anjou, 182
Marlborough College, 34
Marvell, Andrew, 169
Mary, Queen, xv, 3, 4, 7, 27, 59-62, 178
Maude, General, 25
Mendelssohn, F. B., 125
Merchant Navy, 6, 141-3
Mill Hill School, 41-53, 64-67, 111-12, 129, 153-5
Milner, Sir F., 138
Milton, J., 88, 170
Morgan, D. L., 64-66
Morton, Dr. F., 55

Morrison, Dr. W., 131
Moody, D. L., 71, 73
Mott, J. R., 78
Müller, Rt. Hon. Max, 91, 111-12, 125-6, 134
Muloch, Dinah (see Mrs. Craik)
Murray, Sir J., 47, 50, 111-114, 119, 174

National Physical Laboratory, 28
Newbolt, Sir H., 68-9
Nicholl, John, 89
Normand, M., 21
Novalis (F. von Hardenberg), 11
Nuffield, Lord, 122, 135
Nyassa, Lake Mission, 24

Oman, Sir Charles, xvi
Onions, C. T., 112
Oriel College, 131
Osma, Don E. de, 135
Osthoff, Professor, 117
Ousey, Mrs., viii, 49
Owens College, 43
Oxford (see University)
Oxford English Dictionary, 47, 111-114
Oxford Society, 131

Parliament, 2, 18, 22, 34, 107, 170
Pater, Walter, 134
Patmore, Coventry, 86
Panchgani High School, 164
Pangbourne Nautical College, 142-3
Peate, 72
Peel, Sir R., 37
Pestalozzi, J. H., 101
Pounds, John, 101
Punch, 73

Queen's College, London, 46
Queen's College, Oxford, 113, 131

INDEX

Queen's College, Taunton, 162
Quiller-Couch, Sir A., 71

Raleigh, Sir W., 36
Randolph, Dr. F., 124
Ranjitsinhji, K. S., Prince, 69
Ratsey, Christopher, xiv
Ratsey, T. W., xiv, 61-2
Relf, A. E. and R., 68
Rhodes Scholars, 68-9, 122, 135, 159
Robert of Normandy, 182
Roberts, Lord, 98, 138
Robertson, Frank, 61
Robertson, Mrs. F., 62
Rosetti, D. G., 86
Rowntree (family), 41
Royal Agricultural Society, 108
Royal Naval Reserve, 142
Royal Navy, 7, 8, 18-20, 140-1, 157-8
Royal Northern Yacht Club, 62
Royal Society, 12, 28, 31
Royal Society of Teachers, 49
Royal Southern Yacht Club, xvi
Royal Yacht Squadron, 61
Rugby School, 33, 35
Ruskin, John, 86
Russia, 19, 23, 26, 93

Sadler, Sir M., 119-120
St. Paul's School, 65, 67
Salisbury, Lord, 91
Salvation Army, 74-5
Sankey, Ira D., 71
Scotland, viii, 29, 86, 88, 92, 103, 112, 173-6
Schiller, F. von, 14, 85, 90
Scott, A. N., 68
Scott, Sir W., 160, 173
Scottish National War Shrine, xv, 175-6
Seawanhaka Cup, 61-2
Selwyn, Rev., 33
Serena, A., 134

Shaftesbury, Lord, 102
Shaftesbury Society, 103
Shakespeare, W., 87, 101, 171, 173, 180, 183
Shelley, P. B., 87, 171
Sherborne School, 79
Sibly, W. A., 163-4
Siddons, Mrs., 183
Skeat, Professor, 114
Slave Trade, 17, 24
Smirk, Sir Robert, 124
Smith, Alexander, 87
Smith, Reardon, 178
Smith, Stanley, 73
Smith, W. H., 18
Snell, H. E., 68
Spenser, Edmund, 88, 170
Spicer, Sir Evan, 68
Spicer, Gerald, 68
Spicer, Chief Petty Offr., 157-8
Spooner, R. H., 64
Spring-Rice, Sir Cecil, 144
Stanley, Sir H. M., 25
Steel, A. G., 72
Steele, Sir R. and Lady, 33
Stephen, Leslie, 91
Stevenson, R. L., 173
Stewart, Priscilla (Mrs. C. T. Studd), 75-82
Stockton, Dr. F., 47
Stops, T., 160-162
Studd, E., 71-2
Studd, C. T., 71-82
Studd, G. B., 71-3, 75
Studd, Sir K., 71-3, 78
Student Christian Movement, 70
Sullivan, Sir A., 43
Susskind, R., 67-8
Sylvester, F. O., 168
Sydney, Sir P., 36
Swinburne, A. C., 134

Taine, H., 168
Talbot, Bishop E., 70

INDEX

Talbot, Gilbert, 70
Talbot, Neville, 70
Talbot, House (Toc H), 70
Taylor, H. (Bert), 146-7
Taylor Institution, 123-137
Taylor, Michael Angelo, 123
Taylor, Sir Robert, 123, 130
Tennyson, Lord, 35, 46, 86
Thompson, the Brothers, 151-2
Thompson, d'Arcy, 56
Thompson, Samuel, 83
Thorneycroft, 21
Thring, Edward, 43
Timpson, William, 48, 108-9
Togo, Admiral, 142
Tolstoy, Count, 91, 95-7
Townsend, General, 25
Tredegar, Lord, 177
Trinity College, Cambridge, 43
Trumper, V., 64
Tucker, Booth, 74-5
Turner, J. M. W., 110
Tyldesley, J. T., 63-4
Tyndale, W., 167, 180-1

Ulster, viii, 75
University, Birmingham, 128
,, Brown (U.S.A.), 107
,, Buenos Aires, 122
,, Cambridge, 43, 46, 72-3, 134, 135
,, Edinburgh, 103,114
,, Glasgow, 128, 174
,, Harvard, 93
,, Heidelberg, 114,117
,, London, 47
,, Oxford, 8, 47, 70, 73, 111-137, 159, 163
,, Extension Movement, 43
,, Poor Man's, 138
,, College School, 21, 67-8
,, College of South Wales, 177

Vesti, Signor, 154-5
Victoria, Queen, vii, 19, 126, 143
Victoria and Albert, 25, 60

Wales viii, 8, 177-179
Wallis, Mrs. Beeby, 106
War, The Great, 1, 2, 9, 25, 29-31, 51, 70, 129, 173-5
Webbe, A. J., 73
Wedgwood, Josiah, 11-17, 28, 41, 109
Wedgwood, Sarah, 12, 16, 17
Wesley, John, 54, 148, 180
Weymouth, Dr. R. F., 47, 112
Whiley, Mark, 149
Whitefield, George, 148, 180
Whittier, J. G., 95
Wilberforce, William, 107
William the Conqueror, 182
Williamson, H. R., 122
Worcester College, Oxford, 127, 129
Worcester, H.M.S., 142-3
Wordsworth, William, 171
Worldwide Evangelization Crusade, 79
Wright, Elizabeth Mary, ix, 116, 118-120, 126-7
Wright, Joseph, 111-2, 114-120, 125, 130
Wyatt, W. C., 156-7
Wycliffe College 67-9, 157-8, 162-4, 167
Wycliffe, John, 124

Yarrow, Sir A., 18-31, 174
Yarrow, Mrs. (Esther Lindo), 19
Yarrow, Norman and Eric, 29
Yarrow, Sir Harold, xiv, 29

Young, Jephtha, 150-1
Young, Captain, 24

Zaharoff, Sir Basil, 134

ERRATA

p. 69 *for* 'Duleepsinjhi' *read* 'Duleepsinhji.'

p. 73 *for* 'Sir William Grenfell' *read* 'Sir Wilfrid Grenfell.'

p. 43 *for* 'Marion Johnstone' *read* 'Mary Johnstone.'

p. 89 *for* 'John Nicholl' *read* 'John Nichol.'

p. 103 Sir Henry Jones was at Glasgow University, *not* Edinburgh.